CONCILIUM

CONCILIUM 2000/5

IN THE POWER OF WISDOM
Feminist Spiritualities of Struggle

Edited by
María Pilar Aquino
and Elisabeth Schüssler Fiorenza

SCM Press · London

Published by SCM Press, 9–17 St Albans Place,
London N1 0NX

Copyright © Stichting Concilium

English translations © 2000 SCM-Canterbury Press Ltd

ISBN 0 334 03059 5

Typeset by Regent Typesetting, London
Printed by Biddles Ltd, Guildford and King's Lynn

Concilium Published February, April, June, October,
December

Contents

6   *Contents*

Introduction: Walking in the Way of Wisdom

ELISABETH SCHÜSSLER FIORENZA

In the last decades spirituality has become a key topic not only in theology but also in commercialized forms of self-help groups and the New Age movements. The *Wallstreet Journal* reports that spirituality is a billion dollar business. Leading companies everywhere are tuning in to the power of spirituality as they look for the means of conveying company goals and for inspiring their people to do their best in the global market place.

We are grateful that we could gather again in this issue of *Concilium* a broad spectrum of feminist voices exploring different understandings of spirituality and its relations to global contexts of struggle. While there are many different ways in which the multifaceted topic of feminist spirituality could be explored, we have invited the authors to inquire into the links between feminist spiritualities and diverse feminist struggles on the one hand and the importance of human or divine Chokma/ Sophia/ Wisdom as their hermeneutical horizon. In other words, the individual articles probe the possibilities for articulating a political Wisdom spirituality that sustains rather than mutes struggles for survival and liberation. The contributions focus on religious resources for such a spirituality and centre on issues of sacred power and justice. They articulate a spiritual vision that not only expresses wo/men's struggles to survive and transform relations of domination but also critically identifies religious traditions and resources for such a discernment of the Spirit-Shekhina-Sophia's working in different global contexts.

The contributions, too, raise critical questions with respect to the figuration of the Divine as wo/man/female/feminine. They also point to the possible dangers inherent in Christian conceptualizations of struggle and suffering. The spirituality of the Divine Feminine extolling the ideal of the White Lady has a long ideological tradition in biblical religions and is all-pervasive even in feminist spirituality. The Eternal Feminine or the 'Cult of True Womanhood' was developed in tandem with Western colonialism which celebrated Christian white elite wo/men as paradigms of civilized and cultured womanhood. It had the ideological function to legitimate the exclusion of elite wo/men from positions of power either in society or in the churches.

This image of the Eternal Feminine and the cult of the White Lady is a projection of elite Western educated men and clerics who stress the complementary nature of wo/men to that of men in order to maintain a special sphere for wo/men. It has not the liberation of wo/men as its goal but seeks to unfetter the repressed feminine in order to make men whole. Associated with this cult of the White Lady was and is a spirituality of self-alienation, service, submission, self-abnegation, dependence, powerlessness, de-corporalization, and collaboration – virtues which are inculcated in and through cultural forms of socialization, spiritual direction, and ascetic disciplines. In and through traditional Christian spirituality wo/men internalize either that they are not made in the Divine Image because G*d is not She but Lord-Master-Father-Male, or that they will represent the Divine feminine if they fulfill their cultural and religious calling to supplement and complement the Other. In both cases kyriarchal structures of domination are kept in place in and through Christian spirituality and the theological articulation of the Divine Image.

This issue of *Concilium* explores a Wisdom spirituality in two steps. The contributions of the first part investigate particular experiences of a Wisdom spirituality of struggle. Nami Kim articulates social-political struggles in Korean society as spiritual struggles, whereas Mary Hunt reflects on three specific struggles within Christian churches which are inspired and sustained by a Wisdom spirituality of struggle. Ivone Gebara in turn begins with her own experience of spirituality and then explores the spiritual experiences of poor wo/men in the Brazilian Northeast who are not necessarily feminists. She understands spirituality as encompassing 'metaphysical' ethical values capable of guiding people and of giving meaning to their lives.

Like Gebara, so also Diann Neu explores the spiritual experiences of wo/men, but in a United States context. She gives concrete examples of how feminist spirituality and therapy can work together in liberating wo/men from debilitating experiences of kyriarchal dehumanization and stereotyping. Finally, Mercedes Navarro Puerto concludes the explorations of this first section with a constructive probing of a spirituality of struggle. She argues that unlike traditional spirituality, feminist spirituality is not expressed in warrior and fighter images or in mental pictures of war and battle but creatively uses the biblical traditions and images of Divine Wisdom-Sophia. She describes a feminist spirituality of struggle as a boarder spirituality, a spirituality of roads, of public plazas, and of doors.

In the second part of the volume the authors focus on the figuration of the Divine in the *gestalt* of a wo/man, be it that of Chokmah/Sophia/Wisdom, that of the Shekhina/Divine Presence or that of the Goddess. Silvia Schroer begins the discussion with a succinct article on the biblical figure of Chokmah/Sophia/Wisdom and her interpretation in malestream and feminist scholarship. Facing objections against the positive reception in feminist theology, Schroer points to the location of such objections in Protestant neo-orthodox discourses. She goes on not only to argue for a positive feminist adoption of Divine Chokmah/Sophia/ Wisdom not in terms of the Eternal Feminine but in terms of justice and well-being, but also points to the location of a critical feminist Wisdom spirituality in cosmopolitan inter-religious discourses.

Susan Starr Sered in turn points out that it is not Wisdom but the female/feminine figure of the Shekhina that has sparked Jewish feminist imagination and ritual. However, she also warns that the female/feminine Divine figure of Chokmah/Sophia/Wisdom cannot simply be taken over by feminists because it is formed by the traditional discourses of the Eternal Feminine. Goddess thealogian Carol Christ also cautions readers not to accept too easily a Wisdom spirituality of struggle because such a Christian feminist spirituality could be another way of saying that this earth is a vale of sorrows. It also could be an often unconscious but pervasive attempt to ground Christian ethics in the absolute, maintaining that Christian ethics is superior to other moral systems that do not begin with and subscribe to an ethics of struggle. Instead Christ advocates an ethics of ambiguity and gratitude for life and love.

Clara Luz Ajo Lázaro contributes a descriptive essay on the religion of Santeria which is central in Cuban popular culture and religion. She shows that Santeria effects a religious inversion of Christianity as a strategy of survival. Instead of appropriating the symbols and concepts of Christianity, the African Yoruba slaves in Cuba masked their ancestral traditions with the symbols of White Christianity in order to preserve their own religious traditions and categories, to endure slavery, and to give meaning to their lives.

In 'Brigit: Soulsmith for the New Millennium', Mary Condren also explores the interaction of Christianity with Celtic religion and the signifi-

cant role of Brigit in the acculturation of Catholicism in Ireland. She shows
how Christian feminists draw on Brigit's pre-Christian roots, the archaeo-
mythology of her sites, her Christian *Lives*, and the rites to be found in contemporary folklore, and they do so in order 'to bring wo/men together in
search of new cauldrons to hold, ferment and nourish our hungry spirits'.

The article 'In The Movement of Wisdom' by Silvia Regina de Lima
Silva which concludes the second part of this *Concilium* issue details how
feminist spirituality and rituals have nourished and inspired wo/men's
movements to reinterpret the experiences of the Divine in their lives. De
Lima Silva sees ritual and liturgy as a public space, as symbol making from
lived Wisdom experience of every day life. It is a moment to change and live
new relationships with greater respect for life and human dignity, a subversive memory, a feast and utopia, a recovering of the body and bodiliness, an
expression of holistic faith and a community in the lap of Divine Wisdom.

Co-editor María Pilar Aquino completes these variegated feminist
explorations of a Wisdom spirituality of struggle with a critical reflection,
gathering in and sifting through the rich intellectual fare and spiritual
harvest offered by the authors. The ministers of Divine Wisdom have been
sent out to the public places of the global village. They invite all of us to
eat the bread of Wisdom-Sophia, drink of her wine and walk in her ways of
creative justice.

I. Struggle Is A Name For Hope

Wo/men, the Ba-ram Bearers: Asian Feminist Spiritualities

I. Introduction

Regardless of how one defines the term, spirituality has become associated with the search for life direction in a world of crisis. This has been especially poignant since the economic calamity swept over most East and South-East Asian countries after 1997. For instance, while hundreds of small and medium-sized enterprises have closed down, various programmes for the cultivation of spirituality have begun to flourish in South Korea. Churches and Christianity-related institutions have expanded their programmes on spirituality under the slogan of 'spiritual healing', 'spiritual renewal', or 'spiritual warfare'.[1] Simultaneously, other forms of spirituality designed to enhance mental and physical health through chi (energy) practices, yoga, and breathing exercises have become popular in South Korea. As its meaning and form grow more complex and multi-faceted, spirituality has come to include a wide range of life-involvements: from institutional-ized religious practices to 'Mother-Nature'-centred eco-spiritualities, from participation in socio-political liberation movements to the New Age spiritualities.

Spirituality, however, often has been misunderstood as a dimension that can be simply added on to other aspects of life experiences and activities rather than as an integral and constitutive force of a whole life. When it is removed from everyday life, spirituality is easily perceived as an individual relationship with the Divine or as a cultivation of 'inner self' by seeking a change in one's life without considering the complexity of one's relation-ships with the wider society. What, then, would be a holistic understanding of spirituality for those who seek meaning and direction in life and for those who are struggling to survive the devastating living conditions caused by economic hardship, socio-political injustice, incessant warfare, and the breakdown of the eco-system? Can feminist spirituality be such a spirituality that integrates, empowers and transforms?

II. Asian feminist spiritualities

Although there is no singular definition of feminism, feminism can be defined as a theoretical perspective, one which theorizes the experience and structures of wo/men's[2] oppression. Feminism is also a socio-political movement for transforming cultural and religious institutions as well as the structures of domination and exploitation.[3] Creative energy and new insights resulting from feminist struggle have brought about a new focus and new expressions of spirituality as well.[4] Having emerged from and been engaged in the world-wide feminist movement, feminist spiritualities not only revolutionize the myopic understanding of spirituality as individualistic, dualistic, esoteric, and other-worldly, but also enhance various renewal movements that are committed to the transformation of the world. How, then, are 'Asian feminist spiritualities' different from or similar to other feminist spiritualities?

Often, one of the most striking aspects is the obvious diversity of religious traditions, institutions, movements, and socio-cultural and eco-political contexts represented under the canopy of 'Asia'. Although the term 'Asia' is contested and requires a more critical examination of what Asian feminist theologians and others mean by it, many Asian feminist theologians[5] have articulated 'Asian feminist spiritualities' as an integral and dynamic force in life that can sustain and empower wo/men in their struggle for liberation. Asian feminist spiritualities are characteristically wholistic, liberating, concrete, earthy, and community-oriented.[6] Many, if not most, Asian feminist theologians have drawn their resources for 'Asian feminist spiritualities' from the mixed soil of diverse religious traditions, institutions, and movements in various contexts of Asia. While some find resources in female goddess symbols and practices from the different parts of Asia, others find them in various forms of life energies, such as chi and Shakai.[7]

In this article, instead of searching for resources for Asian feminist spiritualities in the age-old religious traditions and practices, including popular religiosity, I will draw them from the concrete and historic struggles of wo/men whose spiritualities bear social witness. Feminist spiritualities that bear social witness are different from the popular spiritualities or various forms of self-help, which tend to believe that an individual person can be free from structures of domination without being affected by them. Although there are countless stories of how feminist spiritualities have been manifested in various contexts of Asia, three examples are noteworthy since they elucidate the power of feminist spiritualities to encourage and sustain wo/men in their struggle for justice and liberation. I will limit the discussion on this to the Korean context.[8] These examples include a historical movement during the Japanese colonization of Korea, the life of So-Sun Lee (known as the mother of the labour workers), and the life of feminist poet Jung-Hee Ko. These examples will demonstrate the multi-faceted ways in which feminist spiritualities bear social witness by integrating every aspect of our life. It is in this understanding of feminist spiritualities that we develop a 'spiritual solidarity' among wo/men who continue to strive against the structures of domination in the twenty first-century.

III. Wo/men, the Ba-ram bearers

The Korean word 'Ba-ram' has various meanings, such as wind, breeze, gale, spirit, breath, and air. While Ba-ram has positive meanings when it is aligned with the Holy Spirit, it often carries negative connotations when it is associated with women. Women who are affiliated with Ba-ram have been perceived as troublemakers in society as Ba-ram creates unexpected energy and change. To be sure, wo/men who have manifested the power of feminist spiritualities through their struggles can be considered as troublemakers. They are troublemakers in the eyes of those who wish to preserve the status quo because these wo/men Ba-ram bearers have generated life-sustaining Ba-ram, have stirred the contaminated airs of exploitation with the forces of Ba-ram, and through Ba-ram have sent out the words of liberation.

Wo/men Ba-ram bearers in the Korean context[9] have not limited their works to those who have the same religious tradition and practice, but have shared their works with those who accept and invite their liberative works regardless of gender, class, religious and regional differences. The following stories exemplify how these wo/men Ba-ram bearers have been agents through whom the sacred Ba-ram has manifested her truth and power for the wholeness and goodness of life.

1. Women, who raised Ba-ram out of wedding bands

In the early twentieth century the 'National Debt Compensation Movement' emerged in Korea with respect to Korea's national debt with the aim of regaining national rights and defending the Korean people and land from Japan's colonizing process.[10] The goal of the movement was to repay the national debt of thirteen million won which was used to strengthen the political and economical subordination of Korea to Japan.[11] While a small number of elite men started this movement, a wide range of people from all social strata responded to and participated in the movement.[12] One of the critical aspects of this movement was women's active and creative participation.[13]

Many women from different classes, regions, and religious backgrounds, such as 'women of Confucian nobility, concubines, merchants' wives, women wine sellers, female servants, and Christian women',[14] participated in and organized various groups in this movement. For instance, married women took off their wedding bands and donated them. According to a public statement issued by one group of women, taking off their wedding bands meant not only a financial contribution but also symbolized their freedom from patriarchal oppression, which was epitomized by the Confucian rule of Sam-Jong-Ji-Do (the three obediences of women: to father, husband and son). Women also contributed financially by saving a little portion of rice from each meal. Other women, involved in the entertainment industry, sold their ornamental hairpins and jewellery. The participation of these women can be identified as the first organized women's activity in the early twentieth century in Korea. For instance, Christian women, who constituted 31 % of all women who participated in this movement, organized four nation-wide groups. These groups of women actively participated in the movement, acknowledging the seriousness of both individual and societal debt, as well as the inextricable relation between debt and liberation. One group of women issued the following statement:

As it is with an individual, a nation cannot preserve its right of freedom when it is in debt. When we sisters, who love our country, cried out for God's help and lamented the fate of our nation, people from all over the country, without any previous discussion or engagement, arose and decided to repay the national debt. How could we not participate in this movement!

Although we women once believed that it was our obligation not to be involved in any public affair, we now realize that we cannot just preserve the old law by staying home. We see that women, who might be different from men, share equal rights with men from all over the world. Although we cannot make much money at this moment, there are things that we can do to repay our national debt. We hope that we can prevent ourselves from becoming slaves, help regain our freedom, and contribute to becoming the best country by compensating the national debt.[15]

This statement demonstrates the connection between repaying the national debt and gaining women's rights and power.

The movement has been recorded as a historical failure due to its weakness in building a nation-wide organization and leadership, and its naïve assessment of colonial power as well as its inefficient method of fighting against the oppressive policy of Japan's colonizing process. However, by participating in this movement women could have invaluable lessons in 'public service, volunteerism, organizational skills, and the power of sisterhood – all totally lacking in the traditional lifestyles of Korean women'.[16]

These women acted on the basis of their religious beliefs and teachings that personal well-being, both spiritual and material, is intrinsically related to communal well-being. Their vigorous plea to the Divine was not separated from their participation in the movement as social witnesses. Further, the life-enhancing spiritualities of these wo/men have demonstrated the possibility of 'spiritual solidarity' among wo/men who stand in various religious traditions and practices by breaking the bands of oppression with the unfettered forces of Ba-ram.

2. So-Sun Lee, who generated Ba-ram of struggle

Known as 'the mother of the labour workers', So-Sun Lee's life also exemplifies a manifestation of feminist spirituality that seeks justice and liberation for all oppressed and exploited peoples without separating the spiritual life from social and political involvement. So-Sun Lee, a devout Protestant Christian, has committed her life to the struggle for the well-being of labour workers since her beloved son, Chun Tae-il, committed self-immolation in November 1970 in a protest to 'protect young women workers' in the garment factory in Seoul, Korea. Lee has continued her work by organizing the Chonggye Garment Labour Union and opening a school for the workers to equip them to know and to stand up and fight for their rights.[17] She has also helped the families of political detainees and stood up for students who have participated in demonstrations against the military dictatorship.[18] Because of her justice work, Lee has been arrested many times and suffered police brutality.

Born in 1929, Lee has lived through the Japanese colonization, the Korean War, extreme poverty, the death of her beloved son, and the workers' rights movement. Despite all the hardship, her faith has sustained her life and her 'uncompromising spirit'. Her faith in the 'Min-jung Jesus' and a belief in a better world where everybody can live in peace and justice regardless of gender, class, religion, and regional differences has enabled her to continue in her struggle against the injustice inflicted upon labour workers in South Korea. According to her daughter, Sun-Ok Chun, when Lee was imprisoned with twenty other prisoners, she even influenced her cell mates, who had committed all sorts of crimes, to be nurtured in some religious faith.[19] Lee, by 'sharing spiritual food' with them, encouraged and empowered these women who also suffered at the margin of the society.[20]

When she was arrested and the school in the factory was shut down, as many as a thousand women workers gathered at the court building and shouted, 'Give us back our mother!'[21] It is dangerous, however, to praise her as a role model for 'the ideal motherhood' who sacrifices her own self to serve 'others'. She is called the 'mother of workers' not because she is by nature more life-giving or life-affirming than men, which is often asserted by the patriarchal understanding of motherhood, but because she took the life-struggle of somebody else's daughters and sons as her own. Her life challenges a widespread tendency of mothers and fathers who vigilantly pray for and sacrifice everything for the success of their own children in an extremely competitive society, while ignoring or not even acknowledging the predicament of somebody else's daughters and sons. Lee is committed to the liberative struggle for labour workers not because she is a woman, nor because she gave birth to her own children. It is because she deeply believes in the equality of all human beings who are created in the image of the Divine regardless of gender, class, regional and religious differences. Lee has been sustained by a life-affirming power that embodies an integration of spiritual and political spheres without separating them as two disconnected arenas in her life. Through her spiritual solidarity, as well as political solidarity, with wo/men who have struggled to survive, Lee has generated and regenerated the Ba-ram of struggle.

3. Jung-Hee Ko, who captured the words of Ba-ram

The life and work of the feminist poet Jung-Hee Ko are another powerful manifestation of feminist spirituality. Beginning her career as a poet struggling with the Christian meaning of salvation and suffering, Ko channelled her poetry to embrace the suffering and struggle of 'women minjung'. For Ko, feminist writing is not a special genre which only women can produce, nor is it a 'feminine writing'. Feminist writing, for her, is a movement that transforms all the structures of domination that oppress wo/men. Three experiences that changed her life and shaped her poetry include the Kwang-Ju Massacre in May 1980, her theological study in seminary, and her involvement in the 'Alternative Culture'.[22] Working as the first editor of the *Feminist Newspaper*, Ko persistently emphasized 'sisterhood'.[23] Many of her poems on sisterhood and solidarity among women transcend historical time, class differences, regional differences, religious differences, age differences, and even national differences. After participating in the 'Post-colonial Poem and Music' workshop in the Philippines for one year, Ko began to see more clearly how capitalism has exploited and dehumanized not only women in South Korea, but also in other parts of Asia.[24] Since then, Ko's emphasis on sisterhood has gained more strength than before. Her poem on sisterhood reads:

Sisters,
Now we are the way and the light
Now we are the rice and hope
Let's put our belief in the wishes of a hundred people
Let's raise the Moon upon the river of a thousand people
On the day when twenty million women lit the light of the wish,
Half of the sky comes back
Half of the earth comes back
Half of the people comes back
On the day when the new history begins,
Let's wake up the river of the silence in your heart
Let's pull out the nail of the oppression stuck in my heart
Let's cut off the thick weeds of inequality in our hearts . . .
At last in the Korean peninsula
Women-baram, new baram, the energy of heaven and earth are
   originating,

Spreading flame
from two to one, from one to ten thousand, to hundred thousand
gathered together
This flame is the flame of equality
This energy is the energy of unification
Isn't this wind the wind of liberation?
Sisters
Now we are the way and the light
Now we are the rice and hope
Now we are love and life-giving power.[25]

Like many other wo/men Ba-ram makers, Ko lived a life that integrated spirituality inseparably with the rest of her life. She believed that Jesus' message was focussed on minjung. God is the God of salvation rather than the God of punishment, and every human being is God's partner in salvation.[26] Ko's solidarity with wo/men, and the deep yearning for a holistic salvation which integrates every dimension of life, compelled her to write powerful and passionate poems that caught and conveyed the wisdom and truth of the sacred Ba-ram throughout her life. Although Ko died young, her discerning words of wisdom still resonate in the lives of wo/men who are moved and empowered by her spirit-filled words. She was one who captured the words of Ba-ram.

IV. Spiritual solidarity

Quoting Gustavo Gutiérrez, Aruna Gnanadason acutely points out that 'when one is concerned with one's own stomach, it is materialism, but when one is concerned with other people's stomach, it is spirituality'.[27] The feminist spiritualities manifested in these women's lives exemplify what Gutiérrez asserts. That is, they have embodied the life of spirituality that shares concern for the hunger of others. The legacy of feminist spiritualities is, and will be, lived out through other wo/men's lives.

    We live in a world where spiritual solidarity among people of different faiths is needed more than ever when the global system requires and encourages individualistic and commercialized spiritualities that deflect people from engaging in the active transformation of the world that values property over life. To sustain spiritual solidarity is not about simply maintaining a vertical relationship with the Divine through fervent prayer and meditation, but participating in global political struggles for liberation. Through spiritual solidarity, wo/men of all faiths can work collectively to change the world, as seen in the various expressions of feminist spiritualities of those women who participated in the compensation movement, So-Sun Lee and Jung-Hee Ko. These wo/men Ba-ram bearers could sustain their life of struggle not because they were heroic individuals who were spiritually 'developed'. Rather, they were able to carry on their works because of the spiritual as well as socio-political solidarity with other wo/men who were also moved by the uncompromising forces of Ba-ram. They were the Ba-ram bearers who embodied a life of spiritual vigilance as social witness with and among people.

Notes

1. Using various means of therapy, such as dance therapy, slang-shouting therapy, game therapy, and music therapy, these institutions have played a major role in 'developing' spirituality as well as promoting self-help.

2. I am using wo/men, Elisabeth Schüssler Fiorenza's neologism, since it includes not only all women but also oppressed and marginalized men. See her *Jesus: Miriam's Child, Sophia's Prophet*, New York: Continuum and London: SCM Press 1995.

3. Elisabeth Schüssler Fiorenza, *Sharing Her Word: Feminist Biblical Interpretation in Context*. Boston: Beacon Press 1998, 3–4.

4. Mary John Mananzan OSB, 'Theological Perspectives of a Religious Woman Today – Four Trends of the Emerging Spirituality' in *Feminist Theology from the Third World* ed Ursula King, Maryknoll: Orbis Books 1994, 347.

5. By feminist theologians, I mean mainly Christian feminist theologians. It is noteworthy, however, that the work of many Christian feminist theologians is not exclusive of other religious traditions and resources in Asian contexts.

6. These characteristics have been articulated by several Asian feminist theologians, such as Aruna Gnanadason and Chung Hyun Kyung.

7. See Aruna Gnanadason's article 'Women and Spirituality in Asia' in *Feminist Theology from the Third World* ed Ursula King, Maryknoll: Orbis Books 1994.

8. This article is limited not only in terms of its context, but also in terms of the resources on which I draw. These three examples of the manifestation of feminist spiritualities in Korea are mainly based on Protestant Christianity.

9. The context of the first example of the manifestation of feminist spiritualities in Korea is the Japanese colonization, which occurred before the Korean peninsula was divided into North and South. The context of two other examples is limited to South Korea.

10. This movement was initiated by the announcement of the prospectus in February 1907, by Sangdon Seo, Kwangze Kim in Kwang Moon Sa in Taegu province.

11. Song-hi Lee, 'A Study on the Movement of Compensation for National Debt in 1907–1908', *Idae Sawon*, Vol.15, 1978, 191.

12. Ibid., 192.

13. Moreover, women's active participation did not begin in the capital, like the majority of previous women's activities, but began in the outlying regions of the country. See Kim Yung-Hee, 'Under the mandate of nationalism: Development of feminist enterprises in modern Korea, 1860–1910' in *Journal of Women's History*, Vol. 7, Bloomington, Winter 1995.

14. Choe Ch'oe Suk-kyung, 'Han'guk yosong haebang sasang ui songnip' (The Establishment of Women's Liberation Ideology in Korea), quoted in 'Under the mandate of nationalism: development of feminist enterprises in modern Korea, 1860–1910'.

15. This statement was written by a group named Chuck-Sung-Hoe. Chuck-Sung-Hoe was initiated by Christian women in the In-choen area on 29 March 1907. The translation is mine. Other statements by various women's groups have similar contents.

16. Kim Yung-Hee, art.cit., 214

17. Yayori Matsui, *Women's Asia*, Zed Books 1987, 135.

18. Ibid., 136

19. Ibid., 137

20. Ibid., 137

21. Ibid., 136

22. *In-Mool Yeou Sung Sa (Women's History: Korea)* ed Suk Bun Park and Eun Bong Park, 327.

23. Ibid., 331. 'For the world where women can be united', 'Let's open up the dam water', 'Women-wind, the new wind is blowing', 'If women get together, a world becomes a new world' are some examples.

24. Her consecutive poem 'Rice and Capitalism' reflects her strong commitment to transform a world controlled by interlocking structures of domination.

25. 'Sisters, we are the way and the light' in *Feminist Newspaper*, 1989, 12, 1. The translation is mine.

26. In her letter, written on 13 October 1985. In *The life and writing of feminist writer Jung-Hee Ko*, Alternative Culture Press 1993, 46.

27. Aruna Gnanadason. 'Women and Spirituality in Asia' in *Feminist Theology from the Third World: A Reader* ed Ursula King, Maryknoll: Orbis Books 1994, 354.

Sophia's Sisters in Struggle: Kyriarchal Backlash, Feminist Vision

MARY E. HUNT

Introduction

In the beginning, Sophia struggled.

The struggle continues, as feminists inspired by her Wisdom seek to bring about religiously informed justice in society at large and in Christian churches in particular. Theo-political differences are at stake, visions of society and church that feminists wish to realize in structures, politics and behaviours. At base, the differences involve spirituality, what I define as the choices we make about the quality of our personal and collective lives. Such spiritually-rooted visions are worth struggling over for those who believe that their faith demands concrete expression.

Women-Church, Re-Imagining, and the World Council of Churches' Ecumenical Decade of Churches in Solidarity with Women are three such articulations of Sophia spirituality. They emerge from different circumstances and they speak in slightly different tongues. But they share a common feminist religious commitment to forging deep, effective social justice especially for women, dependent children and the earth. All three movements have been subjected to virulent backlash as a result of their consistent claims to equality, inclusivity and democratic practice based on their visions of Sophia-wisdom. In this essay I will describe backlash against these movements, with emphasis on my local US context. I will suggest future strategies that emerge from feminist spiritual struggles and the vision that sustains them.

I. Women-Church in struggle

The Women-Church movement is made up of feminist justice-seeking base communities, united in sacrament and solidarity, striving to be a 'discipleship of equals'.[1] In language first used by theologian Elisabeth Schüssler Fiorenza, Women-Church, mujer iglesia, Frauenkirche and other such manifestations around the world are groups that seek justice for those who have been marginalized, a way to be in community for the seekers.

The movement began in the US in the early 1980s as an outgrowth of the Catholic women's ordination struggle. Encountering kyriarchal resistance to changes in the priesthood, women began simply to 'be church'.[2] They formed small house churches for eucharistic and other sorts of liturgies, for community and solidarity. The majority of the early adherents came from the Catholic tradition, where the limits on women's participation in ministry are most overt. But the Women-Church movement embraces people from a wide range of spiritual traditions.

It is a movement, not an organization; an invitation, not a set of teachings or doctrines. Three major conferences in the US gathered thousands of adherents, generating a sense of the whole for those who usually worship in small groups. In Switzerland and Germany, groups gather periodically for worship and fellowship. In Australia, a popular journal carries the name *Women-Church*.[3] In Argentina, Chile and Brazil, the term has been used to describe autonomous efforts to engender feminist faith communities.

Backlash against the movement is widespread. US examples show just how virulent it can be. Women who work for kyriarchal Catholic churches have found that their participation in the Women-Church movement, however peripheral, raises suspicion. Do they really celebrate eucharist without a male priest and/or worship Goddesses, the critically curious want to know. Some women are accused of no longer being Catholic or Christian. Others are pressured to take their children to 'a real church' rather than to a base community. Ordination remains a major sticking point, but the most brutal public struggles have been over women's sexuality and reproductive choice, issues many Women-Church groups have embraced courageously in the public forum.

The Women-Church Convergence is a coalition of thirty-five autonomous feminist groups rooted in the Catholic tradition that meet twice yearly for education, networking and common projects. Members include the Women's Ordination Conference, the Grail Women's Task Force, the Women's Alliance for Theology, Ethics and Ritual (WATER), Chicago Catholic Women, Catholics for a Free Choice, among many others.

Some local bishops have forbidden their local clergy and laity to attend conferences sponsored by the Convergence. Such public bans increase media attention and sometimes boost attendance. But the aim is clearly to reassert, with modest success, their view of church and to frighten into submission those whose livelihood is dependent on kyriarchal institutions.

One especially egregious incident was action by Bernard Cardinal Law of Boston, Massachusetts, USA. He banned the Massachusetts Women-Church group, made up of ten active members with a mailing list of one thousand people, from meeting on any diocesan property and from a neighbouring diocese as well. His reasoning seemed to be that the mere presence of this group on church property conveys the impression that 'the church', as in the kyriarchal institution, agrees with the group's positions on such matters as the ordination of women.

Catholics have no problem distinguishing between the well-known position of the kyriarchal church against women's ordination and the more progressive view of the Women-Church group. Despite the Cardinal's actions, increasing numbers of Catholics understand that being 'church' is not the sole purview of the kyriarchy. Land, buildings and other resources belong to and ought to be at the disposition of the whole church, including Massachusetts Women-Church.

The turf struggle initiated by the Cardinal makes clear that it is not so much what the women's group asserts that is problematic. Rather, what is at stake is that it calls itself and is recognized by others as 'church'. This represents conflicting visions – the kyriarchal view that sees 'church' in all its dimensions as the property of the hierarchy, versus a Sophia-inspired view that sees 'church' as a movement of a discipleship of equals with all things held in common.

Additional backlash came from the New England Province of the Jesuits. At their 34th General Congregation, the Society of Jesus, in a papally affirmed statement, invited all members 'as individuals and through their institutions, to align themselves in solidarity with women' (par. 13). Massachusetts Women-Church initiated a series of public dialogues and private meetings with local Jesuits to discuss implementation. However, when the Cardinal issued his decree, the local Jesuit Provincial instructed his charges to abide by the banning and discontinue meeting with the women on church premises. The local Jesuits complied.

While individual Jesuits might continue the dialogue on property not owned by the institutional church, the women found the men's lack of solidarity deeply regrettable, in stark contradiction to the spirit and letter of their own Jesuit document. Massachusetts Women-Church continues apace with its Sophia-inspired work. Members invite Jesuits and others controlled by the kyriarchy to consider ecclesial disobedience in the form of simple hospitality.

The genius of the Women-Church movement is that, despite such apparent setbacks, it is autonomous and interdependent on justice seekers beyond the kyriarchal confines. While backlash is time consuming and annoying, Sophia willing, it can be turned into educational opportunities. Local parishes, religious congregations and individuals, especially clerics, are invited to make choices for inclusivity and to risk the consequences of their actions.

Further backlash against the Women-Church movement comes in the form of certain restrictions on progressive theologians in Catholic circles. For example, a Catholic feminist theologian who is identified with the Women-Church movement is *persona non grata* in most official church settings despite the expertise she may bring. *Ex Corde Ecclesiae*, the official document of the Catholic Church about catholic universities stipulating that a theologian request a *mandatum* from her/his bishop in order to teach in Catholic higher education, heralds more problems. It is predictable that few Women-Church aligned theologians will qualify, even more likely that most will not ask.

The Women-Church movement seeks to expand and revise the very definition of church. It would include 'the ekklesia of wo/men as a movement of those who, in the power of Wisdom, seek to realize the dream and vision of G*d-Sophia's alternative community, society, and world of justice and well-being for everyone'.[4] We are far from a time when the sacraments of Women-Church, its interpretations and theological teachings, are normative. But in the light of such backlash, and in view of the many possibilities that exist for being religious beyond patriarchal Christianity, it is pleasantly surprising that the Women-Church movement remains strong, with base communities springing up around the world. Its roots in Wisdom who 'has built her house' (Prov. 9.1) mean that it is not dependent on an inhospitable hierarchy, but that it has the will and resources to build on its own foundation.

II. Re-Imagining in struggle

Another example of Sophia spiritual vision is the Re-Imagining movement. It began at an ecumenical conference in Minneapolis, Minnesota, USA, in

November 1993 when 2000 women and men met for an invigorating array of lectures, discussions and liturgies led by feminist scholars from around the world. The majority of participants were from mainline Protestant denominations in the US, with several hundred Catholics and a variety of international participants involved. The conference was planned as a North American celebration of the World Council of Churches' Ecumenical Decade of Churches in Solidarity with Women.

Speakers and participants 're-imagined' family, God, church, sexuality, among a range of topics, suggesting new ways to think about foundational matters. Inclusivity and hospitality reigned, as planners mirrored their philosophy in creative seating arrangements, a rotating podium, and a moving 'centre' in the meeting hall.

For once, Sophia was the primary symbol for the divine. Male language and imagery were simply left aside, albeit for only one weekend out of a two-thousand-year tradition. Her name was revered, her history and being were the focus of prayer and song. People gathered in her spirit. The theological and strategic content of the meeting moved in the direction of full communion among all Christians, deep regard for persons from other faiths, and serious commitment to social change based on a vision of wholeness, plenty and sharing. This proved more than conservative church leaders could bear. It was met with fierce and orchestrated resistance, proving that Protestant kyriarchal church officials understood the power of Sophia-inspired spirituality to transform their institutions.

Shortly after the conference, the backlash began in earnest. *The Presbyterian Layman*, an independent weekly written by ultra conservative Presbyterians, and the journal of the 'Good News' Methodists, another conservative group, sounded the cry that the conference had been a wild event full of heretical teachings. They had help from the Washington DC-based conservative think-tank, the Institute for Religion and Democracy, that now maintains a watchdog project to keep tabs on feminist work. The secular press joined in the fray when the *Washington Times*, a conservative daily newspaper owned by the Unification Church, reported: 'A major point of contention is over what it means to mention Sophia in worship.'[5] Radio and television talk shows, serious newscasts and endless articles appeared in which negative critiques were launched against the organizers and participants.

Backlash was vicious. Some participants reported that their mere presence at the conference made them subject to suspicion in their local churches. Several women lost church jobs because of their participation. Outcry in the Presbyterian Church (USA) focussed on the fact that church funds had been used (legally and with authorization) for the meeting, resulting in the firing of conference organizer Mary Ann Lundy.

Several speakers, notably Professor Delores S. Williams of Union Theological Seminary, were vilified when their words were wrenched from context in order to exaggerate and distort their views. Allegedly, Jesus and his father God were left aside in favour of Sophia. In fact, Jesus was very much a part of the programme, albeit re-imagined with everything else. Far from excluding Jesus, Dr Williams used an insightful treatment of suffering from a womanist perspective to suggest how Jesus might be important. The attack on her and her work was racist to the core.

Why such near nuclear fallout for a church conference at which nothing was said that had not already been written or articulated by feminist, womanist, mujerista and other theologians? I suggest that the real focus of the backlash, as in the Catholic case, was not so much over the ideas expressed, though there was substantive disagreement on this. Rather, it was over the fact that disputed issues like inclusive language, intercommunion, a hermeneutics of anti-violence and other Sophia-inspired matters were considered by many church people to be not properly Christian. Once again it was a turf battle over who will determine the content and trajectory of Christian vision and whether there is room for more than one view.

In the US, the long-standing if somewhat dubious separation of church and state results in a right-wing rhetoric that claims that people are free to believe what they wish. However, in this case, the argument goes within denominations; they are not free to expend church funds for and claim that views that were prominent at the Re-Imagining Conference are consonant with the views of their respective denominations. Apparently the mere presence of so many ordained women ministers as well as spouses and relatives of ministers at a conference that received some money from Presbyterian, Methodist, Disciples of Christ and other denominations gave the impression that such diversity of views was now acceptable. This was the impression that opponents went to great lengths to correct. A conference that began each plenary session not with the 'Our Father' but with a Sophia chant was unacceptable.[6]

Fortunately, the backlash served a positive as well as a negative function. Millions of people who did not attend the Minneapolis conference were able to read about it and hear about it in the media. Books and articles abound.[7]

The Re-Imagining Conference, like Women-Church, became a movement. It is now incorporated as the Re-Imagining Community, with headquarters in Minneapolis, Minnesota. Its many members include women and men who have left kyriarchal churches as well as many who find strength in Re-Imagining for the efforts to change their denominations. A newsletter and e-mail list keep adherents up to date on programmes and projects. National gatherings continue, with challenging speakers; local Faith Labs provide continuing education.

Feminist women of the Presbyterian Church have formed their own group called Voices of Sophia. The vision of a just society and a welcoming church community finds expression in many places as people rely on the power of Sophia-Wisdom to guide us along new paths.

III. World Council of Churches' Ecumenical Decade of Churches in Solidarity with Women in struggle

The Re-Imagining Conference was part of the World Council of Churches Ecumenical Decade of Churches in Solidarity with Women, another group that has felt the sting of backlash. The Decade was launched in 1988 as 'a framework within which WCC member churches could look at their structures, teachings and practices with a commitment to the full participation of women'.[8] From the beginning, women realized this was to be an uphill struggle simply to get the funding, staffing and respect necessary to transform a coalition of kyriarchal institutions into something that was safe for, much less affirming of, women. During the first five years of the Decade (1988–93), efforts were so one-sided, results so scarce, and opposition so effective that women quipped that 'the decade of the churches' solidarity was becoming a decade of women in solidarity with other women and with the churches!'[9]

In the second half of the Decade, the women sent 'living letters', in the form of ecumenical teams, to member churches 'to empower and affirm women and encourage churches to be in solidarity with them'.[10] Through these visits by more than two hundred women and men, member churches in all parts of the world were asked to confront the myriad forms of discrimination that women experience, and to develop alternatives. For some churches it was the first time they had received a visit from the WCC, and it is ironic that it would be women who would initiate such welcome personal contact.

WCC women experienced backlash that paralleled that of Women-Church and Re-Imagining. Excellent discussion, education and worship materials produced by Decade colleagues and used widely by small women's groups were all but ignored at the denominational level. Women who promoted the work were seen as suspect. Questions were raised as to whether the Decade was really necessary, given the 'more pressing' political matters facing the Council and its members.

Undaunted, the women unearthed and confronted many forms of violence against women, including that which takes place inside churches and 'finds theological justification in the teachings of the church'.[11] Likewise, racism against women and economic discrimination related to sex were major findings the women reported. Over protests, the women insisted that these are precisely the issues church should be confronting.

Once the Decade moved in this pro-active direction, it became even more threatening, and less popular among those member churches that do not permit or promote women's equal rights/rites. At the women's meeting before the Eighth Assembly of the WCC in Harare, Zimbabwe, in December 1998, the highly-charged matters of sexual abuse by clergy and rights for lesbian women were discussed candidly. Strategies are afoot now to deal with these problems, but progress remains slow since resistance is mighty. Nonetheless, the Decade as such is over but its work has just begun.

IV. Sophia vision and strategies

Attacks on feminist Wisdom-based social/spiritual movements continue unabated. What sustains those of us who persist in a vision of a 'discipleship of equals', a global community that strives to be inclusive, hospitable and respectful of all of its members? It is the invitation of Sophia, who proclaimed: 'Come eat of my bread and drink of the wine I have mixed. Leave immaturity, and live and walk in the way of Wisdom-Sophia' (Prov. 9.5–6).

Such vision is limited without strategies for implementing it. In these three cases, the backlash is the result of women's rightful claims to shape the agenda and to implement an alternative vision of church. Several strategies may help to stem the reflux.

1. Coalition building

In each case the backlash grew when groups gathered in public assembly to speak in one voice against injustice and in support of an alternative vision of church. Negative responses focussed on the gatherings, but in fact were pent-up rage about and rejection of the power generated by a critical mass of women who are indeed changing the churches.

Next steps require clear, systematic links between/among groups to increase effectiveness. Coalitions, whether on-line or in person, will function like 'her seven pillars' (Prov. 9.1) to unite like-minded groups and fortify a movement.

2. Public conversations

Sophia 'sent out her maids to call from the highest places in the town' (Prov. 9.3). Keeping the conversation public is key. Kyriarchal churches share an aversion to bad publicity, preferring to do their deeds behind closed doors, exacting secrecy as the price of admission. But religion is public activity and needs to be treated as such.

Feminist spiritual communities, including Catholic Women-Church groups, celebrate eucharist on their own terms publicly and without apology. A public voice is the impetus behind the multiple newsletters, e-mail lists and other publications that keep groups connected. It is the antidote for women who feel isolated, knowing themselves to be part of a movement because of what they hear and read. The hegemony of English and the need to socialize technology remain challenges, but getting the Word out, risky as it can be at times of severe backlash, is the best guarantee that Sophia-Spirit will survive.

3. Inclusion of children

A third strategy for Sophia-Spirit is inclusion of children in every justice-seeking feminist effort. After all, Jesus, 'Miriam's Child, Sophia's Prophet,' is the best proof that our children are often able to do things that we cannot, that their fresh approaches and new ideas will add mightily to the mix.[12] All three of the movements under attack focus attention on children, whether in special programmes at conferences, in educational materials and/or in worship ideas.

At a recent WATER Pentecost celebration, children blew bubbles and twirled pinwheels while adults discussed how Sophia's Spirit blows through us all. Those children are growing up with a vivid memory of the presence of Sophia in their lives as the backlash continues.

Notes

1. See Mary E. Hunt and Diann L. Neu, *Women-Church Sourcebook*, Silver Spring, MD: WATERworks Press 1993. The concept of 'discipleship of equals' is introduced by Elisabeth Schüssler Fiorenza in her groundbreaking book, *In Memory of Her: A Feminist Theological Reconstruction of Christian Origins*, New York: Crossroad and London: SCM Press 1983. Rosemary Radford Ruether wrote an early volume on the topic, *Women-Church: Theology and Practice*, New York: Harper and Row 1985.

2. Elisabeth Schüssler Fiorenza coined the phrase 'kyriarchy' to refer to interlocking structures of lordship that frame unjust societies. See her *But She Said: Feminist Practices of Biblical Interpretation*, Boston: Beacon Press 1992, esp. ch.4.

3. *Women-Church: An Australian Journal of Feminist Theology* published by Women-Church, GPO Box 2134 Sydney, NSW, Australia, 1043.

4. Elisabeth Schüssler Fiorenza, *Sharing Her Word: Feminist Biblical Interpretation in Context*, Boston: Beacon Press 1998, 183.

5. Larry Witham, 'Feminist parley jars US churches', *Washington Times*, 31 December 1993, 1. The liberal press arrived a little later. For example, Peter Steinfels reported, 'Female Concept of God is Shaking Protestants', *New York Times*, 14 May 1994, 8.

6. The chant originated in Hawaii: 'Now Sophia, dream the vision, share the wisdom dwelling deep within.' Re-Imagining Conference programme, November 1993, 11.

7. See Nancy J. Berneking and Pamela Carter Joern (eds), *Re-Membering and Re-Imagining*, Cleveland, OH: The Pilgrim Press 1995, for a comprehensive look at the conference and its aftermath. See also Laurel C. Schneider, *Re-Imagining the Divine: Confronting the Backlash against Feminist Theology*, Cleveland, OH: The Pilgrim Press 1998, for a look at the broader context in which this backlash is set.

8. This is the description of the Decade provided by the World Council of Churches, www.wcc-coe.org/decade/, 29.9.98.

9. *Living Letters: A Report of Visits to the Churches during the Ecumenical Decade-Churches in Solidarity with Women*, WCC Publications, Geneva 1997.

10. *Living Letters*, 6.

11. *Living Letters*, 48.

12. See Elisabeth Schüssler Fiorenza, *Jesus: Miriam's Child, Sophia's Prophet*. New York: Continuum and London: SCM Press 1995.

Feminist Spirituality: Risk and Resistance

IVONE GEBARA

Two ways of putting forward some ideas on feminist spirituality at this end of one millennium and beginning of another suggest themselves to me. The first stems from my personal experience and the second from my observation of that of 'other' women. In both ways, my own personality, my personal history, my life choices, my values, my opportunities and my limitations mingle with and intervene in the interpretation I suggest. It is never otiose to remember that it is my perception of the world that gives shape to my reflections and, by doing so, confirms them as limited and partial. My perception is simply one point of view, one interpretation, one expression of a view on the world that needs to be completed with other views.

I take the expression 'feminist spirituality' in a fairly broad sense, though I am situating my remarks within the social and cultural context of north-eastern Brazil. By 'feminist spirituality' I mean above all the ethical and 'metaphysical' values that are capable of guiding and giving meaning to people's lives. On this basis I shall try to explain some aspects of 'spiritual' experiences of women who are not necessarily feminists, although my personal interpretation will be marked by feminist hermeneutics and commitment.

I. Spirituality and personal experience

Permit me to begin with my own personal experience. I am increasingly persuaded of the importance of setting forth personal experience as a means to understanding the personal experience of other people.[1] To recover my past experience, I tried to make an 'archaeological' exploration of my memories. Such a quest is of course selective and limited. It could not be otherwise.

1. Loving your neighbour

Today I would state that the spirituality in my life consists above all in a search for an ethical life. This has been its dominant note, and it was expressed in different ways. I believe it could be provisionally summed up in the gospel command to 'love your neighbour'. As a child I heard, at home and in school, many translations of this gospel phrase into others, correct or incorrect: 'think of other people', 'help others', 'share with others', 'live for others'. This phrase, put into the plural in this way, became a sort of reference point in my life, so intense at times that I felt guilty at accepting some or other gift that I knew most children, especially the poor ones of my age, were having to do without. At other times it led me to redouble my ethical sense in relation to others, so that I could never enjoy trying to get even with others. I sought to be obedient to this ethical guiding principle of my life because in the final analysis it seemed to come from God. The other aspects of religion were always peripheral to this basic 'ethical order'. Reference to the commandments of God's law and those of the church, to Jesus and the Virgin Mary were all subject to this. These 'religion things' were nothing more than the power to legitimize or the ecclesial expression of a tradition that accentuated the need to behave in a manner always guided by the needs of others.

When I was a young adult this same phrase from the Gospels continued to guide my life and to make me take steps to make it more and more concrete in social life. The call to 'love your neighbour' was translated into organized struggle for social justice and therefore as a battle against situations and structures that appeared to negate the presence of love in many people's lives. From an early age love echoed in me as a 'gift' of myself to others so that they might be happy. My happiness was in their happiness. Other people were the compass of my loving. I threw myself into this movement of self-giving, and it produced a greater or lesser measure of satisfaction, along with the harsh criticisms that such a course will always bring. Forgetfulness of self seemed to form part of the dynamic of this love into which I was being initiated. And every time my ego emerged happy in the midst of my loving struggles, my 'guilt' at personal pleasure choked it in an effort to show only the 'purity' of my self-giving to others. I began to realize how difficult a thing forgetfulness of self could be. The strength of my ego was effectively evidence of this.

The 'mechanics' of this spirituality of self-giving made themselves felt as a more or less normal part of my daily life. On the one hand, they made me docile and obedient to a type of social love, especially when the talk was all of the certain victory of justice for all, the slow but steady victory of the kingdom of God on earth. On the other hand, this way of acting made me combative, critical, unruly, resistant to any ideology or even family action that seemed contrary to this love. Nothing that meant deriving personal advantage from a situation or even making use of any gift that was not a communal one was acceptable. Exclusions, injustices, or even things that struck me as less just were unbearable. I wanted to drink from one sole source, the source that sprang from the 'one true God', a source that came to me through this insistent call to 'love your neighbour'. My entry into 'religious life' and remaining in it strengthened the foundations of my spirituality and of my life choices.

To me, this seemed to be the only spiritual route possible, despite its rigidity and the inevitable contradictions it produced.

2. *Personal risk and resistance*

Risking my life for others and resisting selfish interests characterized the spirituality that inspired my life. Encountering liberation theology in the 1970s and feminism in the early 1980s accentuated this spiritual quest in which I had been steeped from an early age. Each encounter brought a different perception and a critical consciousness different from that of my earlier periods.

Liberation theology opened my eyes to a sharper perception of social struggles as ways of being faithful to the gospel and as proclamations of the kingdom of God among us. Feminism, in its turn, made me suspicious of patriarchal religion and set me to seeking justice on the basis of women's particular experience. Once more I was able to gauge the growth of various ways in which people were being oppressed and subjected, oppressions hidden away in the folds of our culture, silenced and shut away to prevent any threat to established power. I began to see that the 'ethical command-ment' above all others, the one that guided my life, had to be re-examined from a woman's viewpoint. This meant going into the process of theological deconstruction of patriarchalism and becoming involved in a different struggle for justice in human relationships. It meant going down a road of denouncing injustices that had never been denounced before. I was living in this climate of injustice based on oppression of the feminine gender, especially in religion, but without realizing it. The whole oppression of women had a sort of culturally accepted 'status'. I had suffered injustices in all the cultural and religious institutions in which I had been educated, but I had not realized that what I was undergoing was unjust, although I had often felt disturbed by it. Rather late, I came to see that even 'loving your neighbour', the key to my spirituality and to the struggles in which I had long been engaged, was wrapped up in a social hierarchy from which I was always seen as 'second' or 'third'. I was not important . . . The first place belonged to men, to other people, to the social struggle, even . . .

Little by little my ethical spirituality became broadened and acquired differentiations, nuances in my love. I was discovering that I could not be the heroine of love, that I could not reproduce learnt models of love without making my inner voice heard, without my deep thirst being uncovered, without my *self* being married to *the other* without cancelling out one another. I discovered that 'love your neighbour' was just one pole of love: I needed to discover 'as yourself'. This pole was frequently denied in women's education, including mine.

'Loving yourself', as love for the woman I am, as struggle for my autonomy, as affirmation of my capacity to think, to live and be, cost me a painful process of resistance in order to be true to myself within a patriarchal institution that humiliates anyone who thinks and destroys anyone who does bend before its absolute truths. Resisting in order to keep my personal autonomy, to dare to think, to take the side of women branded as 'public sinners', came to nourish my spirituality. This means that all these new commitments come to feed what is deepest within me, what makes me be what I am in the midst of the collectivity of men and women with whom I live.

'Love yourself' and 'love your neighbour' derive from the same source and one cannot be practised to the detriment of the other.

II. The spiritualities of 'others'

Who are these 'other' women of whom I should like to speak? I should like to share some brief observations concerning three groups of women with whom I share my life on a close ongoing basis: (1) poor and unorganized women in north-eastern Brazil; (2) women organized in social movements; (3) women religious living and working among the people.

1. Poor and unorganized women in north-eastern Brazil

I am often forced to recognize that my living among the poor is being a foreigner in one's own country. I feel close in my heart and in my life choice, but at the same time distant in the way I feel about things and look at life. I am constantly asking myself what values inspire the lives of poor women living in shanty towns, what spirituality guides their lives. And I am more and more faced with the difficulty of giving a single answer to these questions. These women do not exist as a homogenous group but as separate groups, sub-groups and individuals. Their behaviour and values are varied. I try to understand this very complex world and to work out provisional interpretations.

The great majority of these women are caught up in the daily struggle to survive. And their behaviour in this struggle covers the whole spectrum from competitiveness and selfishness to solidarity, faithfulness and tenderness.

In general, most of these women depend on powerful 'transcendent' powers, belonging either to the Christian world or to Afro-Brazilian religions or to other forms of religious expression, to help them in the difficult task of living and surviving in their degrading economic situation. They all, in their own way and in accordance with their individual needs and convictions, cling to a saint or a divinity. They hope to receive what they need and derive 'spiritual' support to save them from despair. They sustain themselves in their day-to-day existence by asking help from 'heavenly' beings or beings from other spheres, the only ones 'inclined' and 'available' to help them in a society from which any human source of help seems to have vanished. They do not engage in any critical examination of their piety. They live, as they say, 'pushing at life with their belly' and living off whatever enables them to survive. They never use the term 'spirituality' to express their religious values or resources.

2. Women organized in social movements

What inspires these women is a humanist political view of life. They act independently of religious traditions, even if there are still influences of some religion or other in their personal lives, and their public stance is linked to the causes they uphold. Some have had negative religious experiences in their childhood or youth, and they reject religious affiliations as sources of alienation. What actually inspires them is the healing of this or that social 'sore' and the restoration of just relationships. The term 'spirituality' rarely has any place in their vocabulary. Most of them talk of looking for a meaning to life, of values by which to live, of historical and political hopes to be realized. They often feel a lack of opportunities for celebrating, which they see as expressing the values they seek, but they cannot find a way of incorporating it into their work. The struggle for just policies, for women's rights on so many levels of civil society, is not linked to celebrations in the religious sense of the term. The political tradition inspired mostly by 'left-wing politics' fails to concern itself with symbolic times of celebration. At most it is capable of organizing a party with good food and drink and perhaps speeches, without reference to 'inner' or more or less 'transcendental' dimensions of life. Everything is seen in terms of this or that immediate aim. The movement has no 'liturgy', no common fund in which a tradition is collectively accepted and celebrated. With all the failings inherent in any movement, however, these groups do show a sense of service to and solidarity with women's issues that is worthy of admiration.

3. *Women religious living and working among the people*

The movement of women religious belonging to various Roman Catholic Congregations living and working among the people has existed in Brazil for more than thirty years. These women do speak of 'spirituality' and refer to it as a formative element in their lives. Moving on from there, they also see how the word has its roots and development in a fairly restricted religious ambience. These are people organized in Congregations or lay movements, and they are seeking new meanings for a word they use regularly.

The spirituality of these women religious is based above all on the conviction that Jesus was a poor man living among the poor in order to build the 'kingdom of God'. They have been greatly influenced by Latin American liberation theology and by social movements working for a more just and egalitarian society.

At the present time, most of those who make up this movement can be said to be going through a time of crisis and of a certain evaporation of their 'spiritual convictions'. The number of women religious living among the people has declined steeply. Their importance to the local church is hardly recognized. Teams are not renewed. Such a situation stems from the new historical and religious situation in Latin America. The churches have ceased to be the public 'voices of the voiceless' and are presenting a public face more and more linked to mass religious experiences of a Pentecostal type, devoid of overt ethical social content. The 'media' seem to be in control of religious mega-shows capable of attracting thousànds upon thousands of people thirsting for consolation, feelings, and pleasure.[2] No effort is required to follow this festive Christianity: you just have to be bold enough to sing, raise your arms, and try out some simple dance steps. This is a long way from the ethical Christianity of liberation, which required analyses of situations, biblical reflection, and concrete steps in action.

Feminism, for its part, has introduced doubts concerning patriarchal religion and women's submission to male authority in the churches into the lives of these 'religious'. Women religious began to dare to disagree with 'pastors' and to refuse to accept their authority as the word in the faith community. A good number of conflicts arose, and many women were expelled from or withdrew from church activities under male control. This socio-religious situation is experienced as a spiritual crisis. The old certainties have been swept aside and new ones are not yet established. So spirituality has to apply very much to daily life, to the present moment, to celebrations organized around elements not necessarily derived from the Christian patriarchal tradition. There is deep personal lack of satisfaction, but there are no meaningful new ways in sight.

4. The risk and struggle of 'others'

For women of the poorest classes, living is already a risk and a daily process of struggle. When they manage to get through a day in relative peace and with a reasonable amount to eat, this is already a victory. Crimes, quarrels – especially among men – and drug trafficking involving young people fill their domestic and social life with trials and tribulations. It is nearly always the women who have to look after men who have been wounded or hide those against whom death threats have been made. It is they who go to fetch their sons from prisons or public hospitals. Added to all this is the daily violence of hunger and totally inadequate living conditions.

These tragic conditions are so well known and so widespread that they seem no longer to attract any interest. It is as though we put the lives of the poor into a sort of 'closed box' in which it is difficult to move and from which it is impossible to get out. We virtually lump the dramas of their lives together, treating one tragedy just like another. We trivialize daily violence to the point where we can no longer weep at the deaths that take place in large numbers every day.

I must stress that this is my view of the lives of the poor and especially of poor women, giving voice to their pain in my way. I feel their pain from my world, my background and my ethical indignation. It is in this sense that I claim that their daily lives are made up of risk and struggle. For them, this is 'everyday life', and simply part of the 'culture of poverty', which is marked by open and unceasing violence. I don't know how one could speak of 'spiritual' struggle in the midst of this brute materiality of violence. I would rather speak of 'selective wisdom', a wisdom that helps them to find solutions where they can and leave most problems unsolved. Most poor women seem to have learned to live with problems that have no immediate solution. They know how to leave things for tomorrow. They manage to accommodate – even quite easily – to the lack of medical care, the lack of water, the lack of basic sanitation. Despite all these, they find time and ways to enjoy themselves, ways they can communicate to others, ways of laughing at their own misfortune. I confess that at times I am driven to exasperation and despair. Many of my neighbours are even amazed at my anger, my approaches to the authorities demanding solutions to the minor problems of the neighbourhood.

For women organized into social movements, risks and struggles translate into the wider political and social struggle to uphold their feminist convictions in the midst of a society that continually threatens their efforts to gain their rights and respect. They have an ethical commitment that shows in political and social outcomes and makes them vulnerable to many attacks. It is as well to remember that in the past twenty years in Brazil many women belonging to popular movements have been assassinated by groups representing interests contrary to those of the majority of the people. I recall the murder of Dorlinda Folador, formerly a militant in the Movement for the Landless and then Prefect of 'New World' in the State of Matto Grosso do Sul, which took place just a few weeks ago. She had denounced organized crime and the complicity of regional politicians in corruption and various crimes going unpunished.

The religious sisters living and working among the people have also been forced into significant resistance to the established political and religious authorities. Many of them have equally been violently murdered, others have been expelled from their dioceses and parishes, and others live in a state of constant battle with the hierarchical church. Their resistance stems from conviction of the values of solidarity and respect for those excluded by our society. Many of them, as I said earlier, have been affected by the feminist currents of the present time, by liberation theology, and by the various social movements of our day. Their spirituality of resistance is translated into upholding their convictions and their endeavours in the building of new relationships among people.

III. Critical assessment

I find myself in the grip of a strange feeling that will probably shock my readers. I should like to 'rest' the earth I live on and the earth I am so that other things can be born. We live at a time when our life patterns, our paradigms, our theologies, and our spiritualities are tired. We are asking too much of our creativity in trying to deconstruct, re-create, redeem, and insert other traditions into ours. Would a time of pause not be an advantage, a time of personal and perhaps even collective silence? Would it not be a good idea to 'rest' so that the new ideas that could guide our steps, the fresh shoots that will feed our hopes, might in fact emerge? We live in a whirlwind of ideas, of difficult situations, of tribulations and violence of all sorts. It seems that no one is being understood in this vast Babel! It seems as though we are in a collective war, trying to survive at all costs by eliminating others.

This situation makes me think of the biblical story of the Flood. The raging waters have swallowed everything, but in the midst of them floats an 'ark' preserving all the different species of life. There had to be hope, perhaps hope over a long time, before the dove could fly out from the ark and return with a fresh branch, a green shoot, the sign that new things were happening. I take this myth in the form of a parable not in order to insist on the destructive nature of our actions in the century just ended, but to say that perhaps we have to keep quieter, perhaps we have to look for fewer 'spiritualities', so that values that are truly vital can emerge in our lives. I fear that our anxiety to appropriate a feminist spirituality may be vitiated by so many events that destroy us physically and our cultures that we shall not be capable of actually touching the human roots that sustain our existence. Without realizing it, we are beginning to seek to appropriate in a feminine form the elements that mattered most in the masculine spiritual tradition: witness, martyrdom, holiness, imitation. All these still come very mixed in with the masculine models of a patriarchal Christianity of domination and conquest which, although it has helped thousands of people, has also been an instrument of oppression and destruction of as many others. I believe life is inviting us, for a time, to a certain 'suspension' of new spiritualities, to a patient wait for what will come, to a voluntary silence or greater care with our words and our theories. We should not be in a hurry, or we shall find ourselves simply using the same discourse 'feminized'.

In this sort of 'retreat' from theological babble, we should be preparing ourselves, I believe, for a strategy of accepting the newness that is being begotten in the depths of the earth, in the depths of ourselves, a newness full of surprises and still imperceptible to our reason. It is a sort of collective begetting, a hazardous pregnancy with no definite birth date. We are in a time of waiting, experiencing anxiety and even dread at what might arrive, intervening with care just so that life may be respected. All we can do is to protest, through organizations and outside them, at the massive destructiveness that continues to threaten our hopes of life. All we can do is be grateful for the chance to caress our daughters, sons and grandchildren, hoping that our longing for love and solidarity can be the food they receive from us today. But we still cannot even stammer the name of the new forms of hope being gestated. There are not many theories capable of sustaining this waiting. There are just the things that sustain the humanity in us: friendship, affection, solidarity among all, waiting for the new day that will come.[3]

I believe that this is the only possible way forward in a situation of flood and darkness. People need to feel in the first place that there are hands guiding ours, that there are hearts beating with ours and moving beyond the old divisions. We need to know that there are others dreaming with us of a better world. History has shown that this time of waiting in solidarity has in fact existed before and is still in existence. In the near future it will be capable of proclaiming that some fragile 'green shoots' can now be glimpsed. And life, all forms of life, will be able to flourish in the farthest corners of the earth.

Translated by Paul Burns

Notes

1. See the Preface by Adolphe Gesché to my *Le mal au féminin – réflexions théologiques à partir du féminisme*, Paris 1999.
2. Cf. 'A festa no altar' in *EPOCA* 74, São Paulo, 18 October 1999.
3. I remember Dom Helder Câmara who used to say, 'The darker the night, the more beautiful the dawn', to encourage our hopes.

A Voice of Wisdom-Sophia: Feminist Therapy/Spiritual Direction

DIANN L. NEU

May Wisdom be in our hearts and in our perceiving;
May Wisdom be in our minds and in our thinking;
May Wisdom be in our mouths and in our speaking;
May Wisdom be in our hands and in our working;
May Wisdom be in our feet and in our walking;
May Wisdom be in our bodies and in our loving.
May Wisdom be with us all the days of our lives, and beyond.[1]

Introduction

Therapy and spiritual direction are usually considered two distinct
disciplines. Professionals generally train in one or the other field. Some
feminists, like myself, train in both because we believe that women's
spiritual expressions offer insights into how women see the world and
themselves in it, and women's psycho-social expressions influence their
spiritual understanding and religious beliefs. Many women understand
their psycho-social-spiritual selves as an integrated whole. In their search
for wholeness and wisdom, they desire to work with a counsellor who is
knowledgeable of both spirituality and psychotherapy, and attentive to
women's psyche and women's spirit.

Many women seek Wisdom-Sophia.[2] Petra, a church musician in her
early forties, is grieving. Her best friend has just died of breast cancer. She
wants help dealing with her feelings, grieving for her soul mate, and
acknowledging the changes in her life. She is a regular volunteer for hospice
and a member of a feminist spirituality community.

Anna, a missionary in her mid-fifties, feels fragmented. She has just
returned from working in Central America and 'wants to heal some old

wounds'. She requests counselling to work through her survival of child-hood sexual abuse.

Katherine, a seminary student in her mid-thirties, is scared, confused and unsure of her vocation. She wants guidance to think through her sexual identity, ministry, and relationship. With ordination before her, and in a new lesbian relationship, she needs to talk.

Elizabeth, a single mother in her late twenties, has just discovered she is pregnant and is experiencing a variety of emotions. She wants help thinking through her choices, including abortion. She has counselled friends in similar situations.

Maria, a woman religious in her late sixties, involved in health care ministry, needs help with her depression. She is anxious about aging, angry at the church, and sad about her choices around celibacy. She seeks wisdom as she reviews and integrates her life.

These women are similar to others who search for a feminist therapist/ spiritual director to help them recapture their sense of themselves, gain strength for personal and social change, and pay attention to and deepen their relationship to Wisdom-Sophia, a divine friend who struggles with them. Each of these women, composites of clients with whom I work, faces psychological, spiritual and ethical issues for which her religious tradition offers little help, indeed for which it may well be part of the problem. The church musician, missionary, seminarian, mother, and woman religious all sense a need to work with a feminist trained as both a therapist and spiritual director who attends to social justice. Each wants help processing her struggles and her faith journey. All recognize their need for a counselling relationship that enables them to heal, and a companion to accompany them as they work to mend old wounds, experience the presence and grace of Wisdom-Sophia in their lives, and reclaim their wisdom.

This article examines the role of feminist therapy/spiritual direction, describes a feminist spirituality of struggle and therapy of justice, and discusses the therapeutic and spiritual potential to empower women to face and make transitions. I suggest religious resources that strengthen women's political wisdom spirituality and offer ways to reconstruct community.

I. Feminist therapy/spiritual direction

At the time I co-founded WATER, the Women's Alliance for Theology, Ethics and Ritual, in Silver Spring, MD, in 1983, I was a recent graduate of the Jesuit School of Theology at Berkeley, CA, trained in spiritual direction, theology and liturgy. Yet as women and men came to me for spiritual direction, I found their needs not only spiritual but also clinical. Working with them, I realized that I needed more training in psychotherapy to help deal effectively with problems such as violence, abuse, depression, anxiety, growing up in an alcoholic family, compulsive eating, addictions, dissociation, self-abuse, relationships, and so on. So I studied psychotherapy and clinical social work at The Catholic University of America in Washington, DC, to become licensed as a feminist therapist as well as spiritual director.

Connecting therapy and spiritual direction, I ask: How does a woman who comes for counselling experience change and growth? How does attention to spirituality and wholeness empower her to move towards less suffering and a more fulfilling life? What are the socio-economic conditions that ground her situation? What are the theo-political visions that support her struggles?

Feminist therapists/spiritual directors facilitate personal and spiritual development in clients through mutual empathy and mutual empowerment.[3] We believe all relationships – family, workplace, school, friend, colleague and divine – can be renewed by restoring the pathways to connection. We listen to the whole person, psychological, social, spiritual, sexual, economic and political. We pay attention to the workings of Wisdom, both human and divine. We teach the value of women's power. We value feminist consciousness-raising, and sensitize clients to the reality and effects of patriarchy and kyriarchy, especially in this time of backlash. We espouse change of, rather than adjustment to, unjust societal and religious standards, understanding that women and other marginalized persons constitute groups that society has excluded, victimized and degraded. We know the psychological effects of oppression, and we facilitate and support changes in women to experience themselves as fully human: reintegrating what has been dichotomized, empowering that which has been marginalized and abused, and liberating that which has been unjustly burdened.

II. A feminist spirituality of struggle and therapy of justice in practice

Although feminists may differ on particulars about a spirituality of struggle and therapy of justice, common themes shape the feminist content. These characteristics connect women's bodies, spirits and communities in the search for meaning, direction and value for women's lives. They are rooted in feminist experiences, attend to both human and divine feminist wisdom, place women at the centre, reverence the earth and all creation, value women's bodies and bodily functions, seek interconnection with all living things, emphasize liturgy and ritual, act in solidarity with others who are marginalized, and work for social justice.

A feminist spirituality of struggle and therapy of justice sees women as images of Divine Wisdom, recognizing the body as the locus of this wisdom and acknowledging women's birthright and responsibility to participate in shaping religion and culture. From a search for meaning and self-actualization to participation in social change, it moves people to exercise personal authority for their lives and to reject patriarchal, kyriarchal authority that tries to subjugate them.

A feminist spirituality of struggle and therapy of justice is rooted in women's experiences, especially those of disempowerment/empowerment, of resistance to violence and reconstruction of community.[4] It starts with the premise that each woman's story is valid, whether or not congruent with institutionalized practices and doctrines. It concerns awakening to forces of wisdom larger than self and to powers of connection with nature, with others, with Holy Wisdom (or whatever name the client uses for the divine) to effect the equal status of all human beings. It is inherently social, mirroring the 'personal is political' cornerstone of the women's movement.

1. Talking about a feminist spirituality of struggle

Clients often encounter this spirituality of struggle in times of crisis, such as accidents, or natural life events, such as the death of a loved one; traumas of rape, incest, torture, domestic violence; the realities of dealing with cancer or HIV-AIDS; conflicts between religious upbringing and experience, including struggling with a kyriarchal church over reproductive choice, ordination, homosexuality, divorce or clergy sexual abuse; and life cycle transitions. A feminist spirituality of struggle is a force for survival and change. It can give clients strength and courage to face and transform their struggles and relationships. It can nourish and sustain them to imagine a world without violence, where all belong, people care for each other and everyone becomes fully human. It can free them to move towards liberation.

Let us look first at three examples of the manner in which I engage clients, and then specific resources, including liturgy, that I use to bring healing, wisdom and closure to life-altering experiences.

2. Three examples

Petra came to therapy filled with grief. Her beloved friend Barbara had died of breast cancer. In her grief work Petra recognizes and accepts the pain as part of the natural process of adjustment to a life without Barbara. Her grief process is normal and the response of her whole being. I sit with her as she cries, and listen to her pain and loss. I empathize with her as she moves through her grief passage.

Kübler-Ross[5] names five progressive stages of grieving that Petra goes through: (1) denial, which helps cushion the impact of the loss; (2) rage and anger, 'why me?' which she directs at God for causing the loss and at Barbara for deserting her; (3) bargaining, to regain all or part of her loss; (4) depression, exacerbated by guilt and shame over acts of omission in the relationship; (5) acceptance, fully acknowledging the loss, working on alternatives to cope with and minimize it, and restructuring her life. Petra's feminist spirituality of struggle helps her put her life back together after Barbara's death.

Anna lived her life shrouded with the secrecy of incest. As a missionary in Central America she came face to face with violence, and memories of her old wounds returned. Working side by side with Latin American women who had been raped and tortured during war gave her the courage to face her abuse from her now deceased father and move towards healing. I sit with her, listen to her struggles, help her work through her isolation and shame, and empathize with her as she talks about the violence she experienced.

According to Herman,[6] the core experiences of psychological trauma are disempowerment and disconnection from others. Recovery, therefore, is based upon the empowerment of the survivor and the creation of new connections. Recovery for Anna unfolds in three stages: the establishment of safety; remembrance and mourning; and reconnection with her ordinary life.[7] Anna used many strategies for staying out of relationships, including alcohol, drugs and compulsive eating to numb her experiences. She was in terror of being exploited as she had been in the past, yet simultaneously craved relationships. She moved through a long period of fear, shame and isolation before beginning to acknowledge her vulnerability and anger. Anna's feminist spirituality of struggle helps her pay attention to her wisdom and learn to value her body. She works to overcome her addictions to drugs and alcohol, and to control her compulsive eating. Her strong feminist Catholic social justice background helps keep her spirit alive when her struggles intensify and her tears flow. It helps her strengthen her commitment to be in solidarity with the Latin American community.

Katherine's presenting issue is being a lesbian minister in a church that has problems not only with homosexuality but also with women priests. She struggles with being feminist, lesbian and called to ordination. She brings her pains, fears and hopes into the counselling context. She shares the secrets of her life, the vulnerabilities of her loves, and the burdens of her family and church. She talks about Wisdom-Sophia in her life, the spirituality of a lesbian feminist and the stress of engaging in ecclesiastical disobedience. I listen reflectively, elicit her feelings and thinking, ask questions, facilitate the emergence and discussion of her struggles, convey God's affirmation of her sexuality and her partnership, and connect her to Wisdom – hers, others, divine. Her struggle is personal and political. She has to decide daily whom to trust, if and how to come out to others, how to deal with those who reject her as a lesbian. Women in the early stages of recognizing their lesbian identities are often terrified about the possibilities. Those who have suffered sexual abuse may wonder if this experience caused them to be lesbian. Homophobia frightens most lesbians and causes many to become self-conscious, to question themselves. Living with the constant risk of exposure is disempowering. Coming out can mean loss of job, loss of friends, family rejection, ridicule and violence. Coming out is nonetheless an assertion of self. It is empowerment.

Cass[8] cites six stages of coming out: identity confusion, identity comparison, identity tolerance, identity acceptance, identity pride and identity synthesis. Katherine's feminist spirituality of struggle helps her to come out to herself and embrace the goodness of her lesbian self and her committed relationship. Looking at scripture and theology to discover new images of a God who affirms sexuality is helpful for her. She reclaims her power to stay in the struggle for ordination and work to change a kyriarchal system by supporting other lesbian and gay people, especially those called to ordination.

III. Religious resources for a political wisdom spirituality

Religious resources that strengthen and empower clients for personal and global transformation are many and varied. Some that I use include guided meditation, life review, symbols, group work, litany, dream work, journal-keeping, liturgies and rituals. I suggest reflection over a cup of tea, morning and evening meditation, a ritual pause at night to gaze at a burning candle, a jog around the neighborhood to notice the tulips blooming, a walk on the beach, time for painting, music, poetry, piano playing. All of these, and more, make use of concrete and creative ways to contact and transform that part of the person that has been judged, denied or repressed out of necessity as a strategy to survive. These resources provide a means by which Wisdom can emerge.

1. Guided meditation can offer a client a way to imagine her possible life decisions. Elizabeth, a former student, called me long distance to seek counsel. She was pregnant, in need of help to seek her own wisdom so she could make a choice about her pregnancy. She had to decide whether to bring her pregnancy to term or have an abortion. After several lengthy conversations, I invited her to light a candle, absorb its power and relax. I prayed:[9] *Gracious and loving Wisdom–Sophia, fill Elizabeth with wisdom that she may know clearly the choice that she needs to make. Bless her and comfort her with your Spirit.*

I then led her through a guided meditation, saying: *Elizabeth, close your eyes, take a deep breath, and feel your body begin to relax. Imagine yourself walking on a path through the woods. You are walking into the future, your future. At the end of this path imagine yourself in five years if you decide to bring this pregnancy to term. Take three minutes and listen to yourself . . .* (Pause)

Now begin again. (Pause fifteen seconds.) *Imagine another path through the woods. Walk along this path. At the end of this path experience yourself in five years if you do not bring this pregnancy to term. Take three minutes and experience what this is like . . .* (Pause)

Now that you have visualized these two pathways, think of a favourite place where you feel most comfortable, and imagine yourself there now. Take a deep breath, let your body relax, and think about what you have experienced. Take as long as you like . . . (Pause)

I closed, saying: *Elizabeth, do something comforting now. Drink a cup of tea, take a warm shower, listen to soothing music, or walk in the garden. I am with you. Wisdom–Sophia is with you.* Elizabeth reported that this meditation empowered her to experience Wisdom – hers, others, the divine – and make her private decision.

2. Life review can help a client gain an overview and pinpoint issues that cry out for resolution.[10] Maria's life review gave her an opportunity to grapple actively with her history so she could make peace with it by facing the issue of sexuality in her life, freeing herself from guilt and shame, mourn-

ing the choices she did not make, and moving on. It helped her realize that some of her depression came from working with and living in a patriarchal, racist and classist church and society. She could downsize belongings, catalogue memories and address unfinished business in order to focus on self-restoration. She brought the unexpressed pain, anger and grief from her past into the light of day so she could work out steps to make peace with the unsettled events in her life. She was challenged to resolve her struggles between integrity and despair. This life review, she found, empowered her through looking back not for the sake of the past but for the sake of the present and future. She has since volunteered as a teacher with poor women.

3. Symbols can release insights and energy, evoke connection and invite action. I use symbols in individual sessions and group work. When facilitating groups, I put a table in the centre of our gathering and place such symbols on it as a bowl of water, shells or flowers, candles, a pot of soil and seeds, rocks, a jar of oil or other items. About ten minutes before closing the session, I invite group members to focus on the theme and interact with a symbol. After one feminist spirituality group talked about the power of women friends to strengthen one another in suffering and to strategize for change, each participant named a friend who had been significant in her life. Each woman took a floating candle, put it in the bowl of water and spoke a word of thanks for her friend. Petra, who named her friend Barbara, attributed the symbols of water and candles with connecting her in a new way to her beloved lost companion.

4. A Litany can help the client name the pain she wants to release and the changes she is making. Anna and I had worked together weekly for three years. For her final session she chose to write and bring in a litany to give herself the gift of integration and healing. At this last session I lit a candle as a symbol of her transformation and said: Anna, reclaim your healing powers for yourself and others. She read the detailed litany she had written, including:

I release the abuse to my body through compulsive overeating, poor food choices, and lack of exercise.
I release the abuse to my body and soul through incestuous sexual activity.
I release the abuse to myself through unhealthy sexual/romantic relationships.
I release my inattentiveness to the needs and concerns of others because of my self-absorption and apathy.

When she finished, I said: Anna, may you be released from the effects of the abuse and harm that was done to you unjustly and that you did to yourself. How have you experienced change and growth, and how do you see a way to a different kind of living that is life-enhancing?

Anna responded:

I am allowing myself the time and space to explore my life and come to self-knowledge. I am committing resources to this endeavour.

I am learning to allow others to live their own lives and learning that supporting others is not enabling or doing for them what they can do for themselves.

I am committing time and resources to healing my physical body . . .

At her conclusion I told a story of transformation, gave her the candle as a gift, and said: Anna, this candle symbolizes your transformation. Light it to remember your power. When you feel alone know that I am with you. Wisdom-Sophia is with you. May your joy, self-esteem and peace be restored. May you be strengthened to reconnect with your ordinary life. May you go forth ready to begin again. I closed by saying the Wisdom prayer, which is at the beginning of this article, using the 'you' form.

This litany was cathartic for Anna who confided that she felt freed from the past and able to go forward. She later moved geographically closer to her family and became the director of a Catholic social justice organization.

5. Dream work can give a client information about integrating her life. Katherine was visited in her dreams by her beloved grandparents, great aunt and other friends who took turns embracing her and telling her how much they loved her. She received from them gifts of courage, boldness and wisdom. Katherine reported that the dream and her reflection on it helped her feel bolder, wiser and proud to be a lesbian.

6. Journal-keeping offers the client space to record inner reflections, important events, memories and feelings that need attention. Elizabeth journalized about her pregnancy, her choices and her abortion. She recorded her dreams, noted feelings, jotted conversations with Wisdom-Sophia, listed pros and cons for her possible choices, made timelines for decision-making and reflected on conversations she had with friends and family. Writing gave her a sense of connection with Divine Wisdom in making her decisions.

7. Feminist liturgies empower individuals and communities for personal

and social transformation. They provide a collective place where feminist wisdom becomes normative. They offer women a way of consciously recognizing and supporting a life event rather than denying or rejecting it. They use symbols and stories, images and words, gestures and dances, along with a variety of art forms, which emerge from feminist experiences. Their effect is behavioural, cognitive, and emotional, and assists the process of renewal and affirmation. Maria's liturgy, 'Choosing Wisdom: A Croning Ceremony,'[11] reveals this power.

It began with friends creating a circle of wisdom by speaking their names, honouring Maria for attaining wisdom in her life, and naming wise women in their lives. They placed a wreath of flowers on Maria's head to symbolize her beauty, sang and danced 'Wisdom's Circle,'[12] shared a poem from Julian of Norwich and Wisdom 6.12–17, witnessed to Maria's wisdom, then laid hands on her and blessed her together, saying:

Blessed are you, Wisdom-Sophia, for bringing Maria into our lives. You, Maria, are a precious treasure throughout every decade of your life. As you journey through your wisdom years, may you enjoy
Integrity, to make peace with where you have travelled;
Companions, to share your wisdom and your longings;
Laughter, to stay connected with the joys of life;
Challenges, to stretch your imagination and deepen your knowledge;
Solitude, to enter the well of your being and the womb of the universe.
Blessed are you, Wisdom-Sophia. Surround our beloved sister Maria with grace, energy and wisdom. Walk beside her all the days of her life. Let your Spirit, Wisdom-Sophia, radiate through her. Bless her on her journey through her wisdom years as she comes home. Amen. Blessed be. Let it be so.

Maria welcomed this liturgy with renewed energy for the next steps of her life journey.

Conclusion: Reconstructing community

It is not enough for Petra, Anna, Katherine, Elizabeth, Maria and women like them to enter feminist therapy/spiritual direction, change, grow and see their way to a meaningful life. There is a need to reconstruct community, to transform the relationships that breed violence and cause brokenness, and to work for justice for all. Reconstruction demands that a community of people work to find a cure for breast cancer; eradicate violence against women, heterosexism, and all forms of oppression; make women's reproductive choices safe and certain; and value the aging cycle.

A political wisdom spirituality is recognized by others and oneself through its fruits: an abiding awareness of one's own value, potential, and uniqueness; a calm but clear sense of one's own authority; a fierce, passionate stance for social justice; an ability to be authentically, unambiguously present; a capacity for respecting others; a passion for transforming relations of domination; and a commitment to work to restructure community. May Wisdom be with us all the days of our lives, and beyond.

Notes

1. D. L. Neu, 'Choosing Wisdom: A Croning Ceremony', *WATERwheel* 6, 3 (1993), 4–5.
2. Wisdom-Sophia in the Hebrew Scriptures and Apocrypha is God's own being in creative and saving involvement with the world. See E. Schüssler Fiorenza, *Jesus: Miriam's Child, Sophia's Prophet*, New York: Continuum and London: SCM Press 1995.
3. J. B. Miller, *The Healing Connection*, Boston: Beacon Press 1997; J. V. Jordan, A. G. Kaplan, J. B. Miller, I. P. Stiver, J. L. Surrey, *Women's Growth in Connection*, New York: The Guilford Press 1991; M. L. Randour, *Women's Psyche, Women's Spirit: The Realty of Relationship*, New York: Columbia University Press 1987; T. A. Laidlaw, C. Malmo and Associates, *Healing Voices: Feminist Approaches to Therapy with Women*, San Francisco: Jossey-Bass, 1990.
4. M. J. Mananzan, M. A. Oduyoye, E. Tamez, J. S. Clarkson, M. C. Grey, L. M. Russell (eds), *Women Resisting Violence*, Maryknoll, NY: Orbis Books 1996; S. M. Schneiders, 'Feminist Spirituality: Christian Alternative or Alternative to Christianity?' in *Women's Spirituality* ed. J. W. Conn, New York: Paulist Press 1996, 30–67.
5. E. Kubler-Ross, *On Death and Dying*, London: Tavistock 1976; S. Butler and B. Rosenblum, *Cancer in Two Voices*, San Francisco: Spinsters Book Company 1991; G. Westberg, *Good Grief*, Philadelphia: Fortress Press 1962; I. D. Yolom, 'Bereavement Groups: Techniques and Themes,' *International Journal of Group Psychotherapy*, 38, 4 (1988), 419–46.
6. J. L. Herman, *Trauma and Recovery*, New York: Basic Books 1992; E. Bass and L. Davis, *The Courage to Heal*, New York: Harper & Row 1988.
7. Ibid.
8. V. Cass, 'Implications of Homosexual Identity Formation for the Kinsey Model and Scale of Sexual Preference' in D. P. McWhirter, S. A. Sanders, and J. M.

Reinisch, *Homosexuality/Heterosexuality*, New York: Oxford University Press 1990, 248–51; see also J. L. Marshall, *Counseling Lesbian Partners*, Louisville, KY: Westminster John Knox Press 1997.

9. D. L. Neu, 'You Are Not Alone: Seeking Wisdom', *WATERwheel* 4, 4 (1991–92), 4.

10. C.Saussy, *The Art of Growing Old*, Minneapolis: Augsburg 1998.

11. Neu, 'Choosing Wisdom'; see also D. L. Neu, 'Women's Empowerment Through Feminist Rituals', *Women & Therapy*, 16, 2/3 (1995), 185–200; D. L. Neu, 'Wir sind Heilerinnen. Zur Bedeutung feministischer Liturgien in therapeutischen Prozessen', *Schlangenbrut*, 62 (1998,) 23–25.

12. 'Wisdom's Circle' adapted from 'Jacob's Ladder,' an African-American Spiritual.

We Know, We Can: Wisdom and Creation in Wo/men's Spiritual Experience

MERCEDES NAVARRO PUERTO

Introduction: the spirituality of war and women's experience

The spirituality of the West is loaded with metaphors of war. Terms such as struggle, combat, strategies, vanguard, enemy, victory, rout, and the like have passed into our way of understanding and expressing important aspects of our piety. We take their universality and naturalness for granted. Women, who have historically had no direct experience of war, have assimilated the metaphor and make use of terms, symbols and images we know only by hearsay. We have thus contributed to naturalizing and socializing intra-personal, interpersonal, and group conflicts in the form of battle, struggle, and confrontation. We also view many of our own religious and spiritual conflicts in these terms. And yet there are alternatives. Active and passive resistance covers a whole semantic field of which we women have a long and varied experience. The dynamic of process also provides an alternative symbolic field. And the same can be said of paradox, gates, and ways. Our manners of living, of thinking, of loving, and of believing are full of these expressions, images, symbols, and metaphors. It is time, therefore, to put them forward as alternatives to the patriarchal spirituality of struggle understood as a war. In what follows I shall approach the feminist spirituality of struggle not in patriarchal warlike terms but using the images and symbols that derive from *resistance, active knowledge, paradox, frontier, passion,* and *process.* The Wisdom current in the Bible in relation to creation provides a solid support to our centuries-old experience and to our intentions and quests in the present.

I. Creating and creative wisdom

1. Knowing and testing in order to create

No human being has been able to grow healthily and harmoniously without testing reality directly. Every creative expression is made possible thanks to the process, often hard and frustrating, of testing, resisting, renewing the attempt, and expanding one's awareness on the basis of results. Every social success is built on the back of multiple experiences of failure and fear stemming from risk and trial and error. Creation and creativity do not spring from a vacuum but derive from both passionate intuition and long apprenticeship, from persistent resistance, and from the spiral process proper to progressive learning. We women know a lot about all this thanks to our struggle, from the feminist standpoint, to achieve the knowledge, spirituality, and wisdom proper to us as individuals and as a gender. This wisdom is derived from the richness and diversification of knowledge of a wide variety of women, who have shared it by putting it into words. It comes down to us through their risking involving their senses, bodies, and sexuality in the process of learning. Today it all forms a deposit of wisdom for us and for our daughters, transmitted, even if imperceptibly, through non-verbal language, the visibility of our social advances and the atmosphere we encourage in our surroundings.

   None of this, however, has been easy, and we need to make this clear to following generations.[1] Struggle has been and still is the determining factor in consolidating these successes and expanding our creativity. We have done no more than make a start. All over the world there are still many women who have not been drawn into the current of wisdom some of us now profit from. This wisdom is no longer slanted towards conservation, as it was previously defined, but towards creation.

2. Creation in Genesis 3.1–7: meanings, understanding, limits

Women have adopted resistance to death as a form of creation over the centuries. They have made use of their wisdom to oppose the destruction brought about most often by violent patriarchal culture and piety. Yet this feminine effort has left hardly a trace. Our civilization (at least in the West) shows no marks or results of our efforts. Historical research into our ancestors reveals a patriarchate that has robbed women's creativity and originality. Behind the ideas and discoveries of religious and counter-cultural movements that have pushed our Western civilization forward under men's names, there hide (have deliberately been hidden from us) women of superior intelligence, brilliant and original women whose names were virtually unknown until today. If this form of struggle has not worked, we shall have to change it.

The wisdom of creation, we can say, does not consist in preserving life at any cost or any sort of life. It is not worth our while for women to go on devoting our talents and vital energy, our intelligence and creativity, to a task of mere resistance that, in the short term, turns out to be conservative and preserving of the status quo, which is always unjust to the weakest, lost, and marginalized of both sexes. It is a useless waste of energy, which, furthermore, narrows our minds.

In the account of creation in Genesis (3.1–7),[2] in the Yahwist document (J) and its Wisdom background,[3] when the woman eats the fruit of the tree perceived by all the dimensions of her person, we find alternative keys derived from her whole process:

– the woman wants to live fully and for ever transgressing the limits and norms that, presumably, preserve from death. Creation (limited by death), knowledge, wisdom, and life are not possible except through *paradox*: living and dying. Wisdom consists in knowing how to create and knowing how to destroy: the new is not possible without the death of the old;

– access to wisdom knowledge comes through an integral *process* in which very many (or as many as possible) dimensions of the person intervene: desire (to test), as the driving force; the senses, which channel and diversify perception (beautiful and good to eat); intelligence, which measures and evaluates; curiosity, which motivates action; action, which crowns the process of choice and selection;

– the woman, for the first time for a human being, can choose because there are options and rules behind her. To create, an atmosphere of freedom is essential, which implies a *frontier* situation and, consequently, the palpable presence of limits and the physical tension that processes and expresses the risks of the situation.

Up till now we women had not had the possibility of following in the footsteps of the primordial woman, the mythical Eve, but now there can be no further excuse. We can create a spirituality based on the wisdom of this woman in her process of learning, and, thanks to this, her access to human maturation. From that moment, when she eats the fruit of the tree of knowledge of good and evil, with her eyes open to her own transformation, conscious of individual and gender differences, she can become the interlocutor of Yahweh, and later, outside the garden, she can co-create with Yahweh.[4]

Today very many women have incorporated (there is no better term) sensory, sensual and cognitive learning into their religious quest. Many of these experience a new spirituality in frontier areas where a real expansion of consciousness takes place. The spiritual wisdom of women has become very differentiated in their learning, interpreting, speaking and acting. With all this a gender solidarity is being built up step by step; ever more diversified and compact, this includes the most marginalized strata of human society. The body is no longer alien to religious experience – not that it ever really was, but it was suppressed from consciousness owing to a dualistic-polar anthropology – and nor are feelings, sensuality and sexuality, or the cognitive dimension and reasoned learning, because spiritual experience takes in the whole personality and not just some of its dimensions. By the same token, commitment to justice and liberation is brought in also, as are political and economic dimensions as well as relational and affective ones. (Western women have been accused of syncretism or even snobbery for incorporating expressions of other cultures into some religious rites. But this can be looked at in other ways: the inclusion of marginalized and repressed elements from other cultures and devotions can be seen as a form of solidarity, for example. There is certainly a risk, but what about the risk inherent in westernizing the religious sense of other cultures?) Religious experience, as psychology of religion well knows, is the most wide-reaching and holistic of all typically human experiences.

II. Available wisdom: streets, squares and gates

1. A discounted yet powerful wisdom

All cultures have a fount of creative wisdom and all people have their own potential. There is at present a large number of self-help books and manuals being written by and for women (so large that I am not going to attempt a bibliogrpahy) – not that they are exclusive to women, but because it is women who are devoting time and effort to searching for themselves and for the meaning of life. Not all this body of writing is of equal value, but it cannot all be written off as New Age and commercial demand. Discounting it *en bloc* and in advance as a feminine sub-genre smacks of patriarchal manipulation, because it ignores the quest while surreptitiously making use of its more valuable insights. (I suspect this because I have seen women's writings on these subjects then recycled by male psychologists, who enjoy credibility and prestige for bringing women's intuitions into line with academic language and scientific structures. Once again men are becoming robbers of women's discoveries to their own profit. This is also true of male and female theologians!) These written expressions – not to mention courses, retreats, institutes, clinics – represent an area of women's spirituality that is then interpreted and adapted by each religious confession in its own way. The manipulation to which this underground current of and potential for women's spirituality is subjected is resisted in various ways. For example:

– most women professionals, writers and publishers deliberately ignore academic and orthodox criticisms: they do so for mainly economic reasons, but the results can be seen in women's groups, religious or otherwise;

– some respected professional women are endorsing the insights in their writings (usually keeping their academic qualifications quiet at first) and so lending prestige to the more popular products, in a process contrary to the usual course.

The problem in this area, as in others, is the *a priori* discounting of our gender, even if its methods and results are widely adopted and deeply valued.[5] The fact is, when all is said and done, that there is a creating and creative spiritual wisdom that is empowering women. And what is new about it is its availability: it is within everyone's reach, in the streets, in the squares, and in places where no one would expect to find it. This is the surprise factor, which our patriarchal society is not recycling – perhaps because it has not even sighted it. Surprising, but not new.

2. The availability of wisdom in creation: Wisdom 6.12–22

In the poem in praise of women in Wisdom 6.12–22, many women find elements and images that are familiar and proper to them: wisdom appears when she intuitively knows she is wanted; she sits at the gate waiting to be found; she appears to people in their paths, visible but not pushing, seeking those who search for her. In this way, wisdom for Israel is accessible to all sorts of people. She does not occupy the chairs of the Torah or take refuge in temples, she does not allow herself to be influenced by race, gender, class or wealth, or by intellectual (rational) ability. The poem describes her in the shocking terms of a sexual worker, whose image of accessibility is, by any standards, most eloquent.

In present-day terms it provides us with a reference to theology from the category of gender. Women redefine theology in terms of accessibility and universality and seek to liberate it from academic confines, which in most cases do not even provide a creative atmosphere but one of vain attempts at conservation.

Like the wisdom-woman figure in the poem, women's theological reflection and spiritual experience are accessible in public places, which is enough to bring suspicion on them. What are they doing in the less desirable sites of our world and society? How come they are not ashamed to expose themselves and put forward their wares, to worm their way in and stand alongside cut-price merchandise? Has theology, which for centuries was the axis around which science, order, life, and creativity turned, the unique and credible guarantor of divine order in the universe, fallen so low? It's fallen into the hands of women – say no more! Many men theologians (and some women ones), who have not empathized with the new categories, write with sadness and nostalgia of the degradation of theology now that women have gained access to it.

But just as Israel's wisdom was able to renew the Torah in terms of relevance, so women's theological reflection at the gates, in streets and squares and on paths, is finding new categories and language in which to renew itself creatively by bringing men and women a possibility of believing within and through the bowels of our world and not beside or above it. The creative and creating spirituality of women can be understood today as a new phase of the incarnation of God in Jesus. No period of history since the first century of our era has witnessed such drastic changes as ours, and the faith now being experienced and reflected on by women, since it adopts and recreates categories that express this situation, is a new step forward in the mystery of the incarnation testified to by the evangelists.

This spirituality is developing within a process of spiral 'retro-alimentation' with the bowels of existence. Its movement is from within and from without. And, like the woman-wisdom, it does impose itself by force or try to win converts by the weight of its argumentation. It makes its way through the authority of the truth it proposes and offers to those who perceive it. Its presence is becoming ever more visible and open. One only has to look at each of the continents.

III. Paschal wisdom: victory over fear

1. A frontier spirituality

Expansion of levels of consciousness brings with it a broadening-out of spheres of freedom and so of responsibility, which includes risks. A spirituality of street, square and gateway is a *frontier* spirituality. And the frontier is an awkward place, a marginal space often seen as no-man's-land – or its opposite, everyone's land. This is why this spirituality and the theological reflection of many women, as individuals or in groups, is attacked by fear. And fear paralyses a struggle understood as *process* and search. It blurs clear vision, slows thinking processes, and inhibits affective ones.

But what are women afraid of, and why? Some years ago psychologists (of both genders) used to talk about fear of success. This is no longer women's major fear. Women are, paradoxically, most afraid of their own power. When they wake up to life and discover what this can give them of itself, they are disconcerted, to an extent that in many cases produces psychosomatic symptoms that express the anxiety producing them. They are simply not managing this situation. This is paradoxical, because they are not frightened into this sort of paralysis by things that ought to frighten them: the realities of pain, sickness, oppression, affliction, poverty, fatigue, work, death, and so on. These they know how to manage. It is not surprising then that among the poorer classes a spirituality based on these central realities still flourishes.

The experience of faith and theological reflection have both been greatly enriched by this aspect of reality, and it has impelled many women to make claims and take up causes of all sorts, from the just sharing of human resources to the oppression of women. But it has also dangerously skewed spirituality and theological reflection. It is not surprising that a spirituality of suffering and death should predominate over one of life and pleasure. And the latter is precisely the spiritual and theological outlook that produces most fear in women themselves – and in some men.

2. Were the women afraid at Easter? Mark 16.1–8

As a point at issue, let me take the scene of the empty tomb, which closes and ends (the shorter version of) Mark's Gospel with the word *phobos*, fear, applied to the women. Because they are afraid, they do not pass on the news of Jesus' resurrection announced to them by the young man in the tomb.

What does their fear express and signify? Much has been written about this, and here I can only draw attention to some aspects by relating and comparing them to the fear shown by the disciples throughout Mark's Gospel.[6] The men disciples express their fear when faced with situations such as Jesus' power over the forces of nature and all that involves his passion, suffering, and death. However much Jesus speaks to them of pain and death, they hear only talk of resurrection, putting the rest out of their minds from fear. Their reactions of asking for power and respect, their claims to glory in Jesus, are defence-mechanisms against this fear.

The women disciples are brought in at the close, when Jesus' death and burial are taking place (cf. Mark 15.40–41, 47). Mark does not mention fear here. But then, in his resurrection scene (16.1–8), terror seizes and dominates the women and prevents them from speaking. It sets them moving, but in a paradoxical flight. What makes them so afraid? They went with certain expectations and were faced with something unexpected that alters their thinking. They, unlike the men disciples, listen only to pain and death, not realizing that these are not the end of everything, that life can burst forth with greater power. The men fear pain and death because these are not the spheres of life men manage; for generations they have been used to the places where a recognized form of life has held sway – public life, which lasts beyond individual deaths. Women, who have for generations been used to operating on the margins of death and life, in a world of limitations, lacks and sorrow, fear the explosion of this other life extending beyond death, which predominates in the public sphere and is allied to pleasure, prestige, leadership and power. The resurrection, by showing them a fuller life, alters the outlook of these women disciples and witnesses, as women. Their first reaction is to flee. But watch for the paradox in their flight: the tomb is already an empty and meaningless place. From this moment on women are invited to re-read Mark from other angles.

Jesus' resurrection is also a strong and potent invitation to women to share in life in all its forms, to overcome their fear of a faith that impregnates the layers of life apparently least amenable to their devotion, such as celebration, joy, pleasure, leadership, public life, confidence in their own voice and words . . . This invitation is still operative and necessary. One of the strongest challenges to women's emergent spirituality, which many women are already taking into account, is a spirituality and theology of life and pleasure. Vitality and pleasure, as women paradoxically know, contain a serious and profound wisdom, freedom, search and discovery, fullness and dissatisfaction. In these we find that, also paradoxically, spirituality is within the reach of all, women and men.

Conclusion

Wisdom, creation and spirituality seem to be difficult terms to relate to the idea of struggle. But this applies only if we follow patriarchal patterns. Struggle, as it is understood today in many feminine and feminist circles, means a persistent, resistant, risk-taking and ever-discerning form of gaining access to diversified, plural, networked understanding of reality. The struggle for a spirituality originating with women is malleable and plastic, changing and subversive even when it appears to be meek. This plastic malleability is the work of wisdom – probing, risking, sitting on the frontier and never ceasing to question, however painful the process. And this wisdom creates a new consciousness, more human forms of inclusivity and solidarity, of justice and liberation. The challenge is still how to overcome fear, which creeps in unobserved and can be perceived only in its manifestations. But fear is, obviously, a human experience that belongs to Easter. Freeing ourselves from fear is a lifelong task and requires us to take it into account instead of trying to ignore it or deny it.

Translated by Paul Burns

Notes

1. According to Spanish statistics, feminist militancy among young people is non-existent. The reasons for this are alarming: adolescents and young people see no need to struggle; they regard the gains made as irreversible.
2. I am not making an exegesis of the biblical texts here, but I draw freely on my own exegetical studies as sources of reference.
3. I have developed this in *Barro y aliento. Exégesis y antropología narrativa de Gn 2–3*, Madrid 1993.
4. Behind Cain, derived from *qnh*, and the interpretation of Eve, 'because I have formed [created] her from God' (as the verb is translated in Prov. 8.22), we find an evocation of mother goddesses, as the account of Eve brings out. See my 'El hombre llamó a su mujer Eva (Gn 3.15–20)' in *EphMar* 46 (1996), 9–40.
5. Some of the leading feminist theorists in Spain have made a detailed investigation of this question in terms of its major themes, such as power, equality, pacts among women . . . Cf. A. Valcárcel (ed), *El concepto de igualdad*, Madrid 1994;

R. M. Rodríguez Magda, 'Las filosofías de la diferencia' in ibid., 109. By contrast, ways of taking on difference by those in power are (a) exclusion, (b) control, (c) differential assumption, and (d) reducing to insignificance.

6. I have developed this in 'Jesús, Hijo de Humano. Don nadie o el honroso deshonor de servir' in I. Gómez-Acebo, *Y vosotras ¿quién decís que soy yo?*, Bilbao 2000.

II. Praise Her From Whom All Blessings Flow

The Justice of Sophia: Biblical Wisdom Traditions and Feminist Discourses

SILVIA SCHROER

I. The problem in the history of research

Since the 1970s, feminist theologians have studied personified Wisdom in the Hebrew and Greek texts of the First Testament and the traces of this Wisdom in the life and death of Jesus of Nazareth or the interpretation of that life and death. The main reason for this great interest has been that Chokmah/Sophia beyond question documents attempts by the post-exilic Jewish and later Christian communities to speak of God and also of Jesus in female images, which have come to incorporate on the one hand the goddess traditions of the biblical environment that have been heavily suppressed and on the other Israelite images of women.[1] Recently the first enthusiasm has given way to critical questions about the biblical wisdom tradition. As Christl Maier has shown, the figure of personified Chokmah in the framework of the book of Proverbs cannot be detached from her problematical counterpart, the 'alien woman'.[2] As we shall see, Angelika Strotmann warns against 'anti-Jewish' traps in Wisdom christology, above all against the uncritical reception of the threats of judgment against Israel which can be found in the Q logia.[3]

Luise Schottroff formulates fundamental, above all socio-critical questions.[4] She recognizes an unbridgeable gulf between the 'gospel of the poor', which she sees anchored only in the prophetic tradition, and the concern of the post-exilic Wisdom writings also to give male members of a prosperous and educated society instructions for a life in Wisdom. For Schottroff, the starting point of a feminist theology of Wisdom must have lain in the preaching of the gospel to those who had no responsibility for themselves and were uneducated, because in patriarchal cultures women and children in particular were regarded as not being responsible for themselves, and being uneducated.

Dorothee Sölle has brought together her suspicions in a programmatic article, 'Wisdom in no way goes with the Prophetic Tradition',[5] much more sweepingly than Luise Schottroff. In view of the fact that today managerial circles too are very receptive to 'wisdom' of every kind, the central question for feminist theology must in fact be the relationship between wisdom and righteousness. In order to get a step further in this discussion, in this article I want first of all to locate feminist grappling with wisdom in the history of exegetical and theological research in the twentieth century – which has been largely Protestant.[6]

With the rediscovery of the cultures of the ancient Near East, the nineteenth century confronted biblical scholarship with new facts to which it was slow to react. Hermann Gunkel, the founder of the 'History of Religions School', was one of the first to investigate the influence of Babylonian creation myths on biblical texts and in a sophisticated way argued that the evidence from ancient Near Eastern religion should be respected theologically, since in it we can hear the primal ancestors of Israelite religion. Although the extremist distortion of the positions of the 'History of Religions School' did enormous damage in the so-called Bible-Babel dispute, research into the affinity between the traditions of the ancient Near East and the biblical traditions continued. Thus, for example, Adolf Erman discovered that Prov. 22.17–24.34 is dependent on the Egyptian Wisdom of Amenemope.

With rising nationalism and the First World War the religious universalism of the turn of the century came to a premature end. The dialectical theology of Karl Barth and others was the first to react to it theologically, opposing to the irrational forces of its time the uniqueness of Israel and the Christ event, a revelation breaking in from above. Only such a theology could offer protection against the commandeering of religion by National Socialism. In the name of the Absolute it engaged with the absolutist gestures of the powers of its time. This theology, the disciples and descendants of which stamp the dominant exegesis to the present day, saw the Word of God mediated by the prophets, history and the exodus as the centre of revelation and faith. The creation and wisdom traditions, in which what was specifically Israelite was presumed to be less easy to grasp, faded completely into the background. Only in the 1960s and 1970s did scholars begin to turn to them again at all.[7] The connection between the creation and wisdom traditions is causal, as the ordinances grounded in the creation are the same as those which are detected by the wise men when they give instructions for a successful life. The affinity is also evident from the fact that in these traditions, deities specific to a region or people retreat in favour of a creator God, and both are international. Moreover, common to both creation theology and wisdom theology is an immediate accessibility, since they both begin from universal experience, the created world or everyday life.

Despite the gradual rediscovery of the wisdom traditions, so far in German-language theology their theological dignity has not yet been sufficiently restored. In the wake of dialectical theology there is still profound scepticism about the value of the biblical wisdom traditions. This scepticism is certainly more marked in Protestant than in Catholic circles, but it has not decisively been removed from Catholic theology, which refers to a canon that is enriched with numerous Greek Wisdom writings. This scepticism maintains a largely artificial contrast between creation/wisdom and history/liberation/redemption; it postulate an insuperable gulf between these opposites and, following the early Gerhard von Rad, regards the Old Testament creation theology as an inessential phenomenon which is either non-Israelite or late. It puts creation or wisdom completely at the service of the programme of liberation.[8]

Here in particular we find the basis for the aversion of Protestant theologians like Luise Schottroff to (feminist) wisdom theology. These legitimate questions are far from being settled. But perhaps we can now recognize more clearly what the task of feminist theology is, namely to break through the theological fixations mentioned above. The Kethubim (Writings) are just as much part of the Jewish tradition as the Torah (Law) and Nebiim (Prophets). A Christian theology which refers one-sidedly only to prophecy, or promises it only the full authority of the Word of God, is at least open to the suspicion of narrowing down the Jewish tradition. The consequences of such exclusions gradually become evident when Christian women theologians bracket off 'Jewish' belief in the law. But a fundamental underestimation of books like Proverbs, Job or Koheleth, for whatever reasons, seems to me to be just as problematical. Moreover it is short-sighted to investigate the impetus of the Jesus movement only within the framework of prophetic tradition, since the Gospels constantly refer to motifs from wisdom and beyond doubt (also) depict Jesus as someone teaching wisdom among the people. Christian feminist theology at the beginning of the third millennium must not take on the black-outs of the dominant theology. Its criticism should be formulated by grappling with the biblical tradition, not *a priori* or from an undeclared canon within the canon.

II. Wisdom is the inside of righteousness: Chokmah as the heiress of Maat

We remain with the question of the connection between wisdom and righteousness. As an Old Testament scholar, I am surprised that these two entities in particular are regarded as exclusive, when in the biblical tradition there is explicitly a very close connection between them, in a great variety of texts. The central theme of proverbial wisdom, many psalms or the book of Job is the way of life of the righteous as opposed to that of the evildoers and fools. All these writings ask indefatigably about the connection between action and consequences, in other words about the foundations of ethical conduct. Even when this connection breaks, the search for the divinely created order of the world and the possibility of nevertheless living wisely and righteously in this world goes on (Job, Kohelet). The late book of Wisdom still has the heading, 'Love righteousness, you who rule the earth.' A *zadiq* is always also gifted with wisdom (Ps. 37.30; cf. Prov. 10.31).

The mouth of the righteous brings forth wisdom;
and his tongue speaks justice.

Wisdom is indispensable for knowing justice, speaking justice, living a straight life (Prov. 1.2f.; 8.1–21). According to Deut. 4.5f. the wisdom and insight of a people manifests itself in concrete legislation (cf. Jer. 8.8–9). Above all the kings whose concern it is to secure righteousness for the wretched and poor are dependent on the gift of wisdom (Prov. 8.15). That is true of Solomon (I Kings 3.28) and also of the righteous rulers of the coming time of salvation who are longingly awaited (Isa. 11.1). In post-exilic texts, personified Chokmah in the form of a woman takes the place of these royal figures as the one who proclaims righteousness.

In terms of the history of religion, the close connections between wisdom and righteousness in general and the image of personified Chokmah strikingly goes back to notions from ancient Egypt at the centre of which stands Maat, the Egyptian goddess of right order.[9] Maat comprehends the divine and nature, the kingdom, society and human relationships; Maat stands for the cosmic and divinely willed, i.e. ideal cultural order. As a goddess she belongs to the Egyptian pantheon, but she holds a special position in it, as the other deities are orientated on her as a cosmic principle. She is present as a witness at the judgment of the dead, as she represents the order for the preservation of which the dead have to justify themselves at the judgment in the other world. She is regarded as the daughter of the sun god Re, though he has to fulfil the cosmic order of the course of the sun decreed by Maat. She is the guardian and patron of the monarchy, just as the king is the guarantor of the divinely-willed cosmic and social order which makes human life possible in the first place. Therefore in the cult the king offers Maat as a gift for the gods, i.e. he accomplishes Maat as her representative and guarantor; the gods do not involve themselves directly in the course of things. The opposite to Maat is Isfet, the state of lawlessness, violence and oppression. The social order represented by Maat is not democratic but hierarchical. But the law for which she stands is the law which gives the weaker a chance, the idea of a vertical solidarity with those who are better off with all parts of society.

Like Egyptian Maat, Old Testament Wisdom cannot be separated from the idea of a comprehensive just order and doing righteousness. The Israelite terms *zedek/zedaqah* indeed often refer to social aspects of justice, but they embrace many further notions of the divine ordering of the world, including the cosmic and natural orders. Like Maat, Chokmah embodies these basic ordinances. Biblical texts also presuppose the mutual dependence of the harmony of social and cosmic orders. If justice is corrupted, a drought breaks out over the land (Hos. 2.4f.), YHWH's emissary restores righteousness and the whole order of creation is restored (Isa. 11.1–9). The book of Job leads its main figure out of the narrowness into which suffering drives him into the breadth of the divine creation. The book of Wisdom imagines that at some time, with the help of the whole of creation, God will wage war against the fools and the godless (Wisd. 5.14–23).

III. Biblical criticism of the wisdom of the wise

The biblical wisdom books are primarily interested in the right order of social relations and other basic orderings of the world. Some wisdom texts resemble prophetic texts in the acuteness of their analyses, which attack social abuses. This is the case for example with Job 24, where the impoverishment of the people of Judah with absolutely no means at all after the exile by those in a better situation is bluntly said to be a scandal, or Sirach 34.24ff., the text which opened the eyes of Bartolomé de las Casas to the injustice of the conquest of Latin America.

Like one who kills a son before his father's eyes
is the man who offers a sacrifice from the property of the poor.
The bread of the needy is the life of the poor;
whoever deprives them of it is a man of blood.
To take away a neighbour's living is to murder him;
to deprive an employee of his wages is to shed blood.

Beyond doubt the wisdom literature that we have came into being in the educated, i.e. well-to-do, circles of Israel, but in principle we can reckon with such processes in all biblical literature, in narratives, laws, songs or prayers. As in Egypt, a popular form for wisdom writings is that of the experiential teaching of a father-teacher given to a pupil-son. Court officials who held the office of counsellor were regarded as professional 'wise men'. Nevertheless the material from which Psalms, Proverbs or the Book of Job has been created is traditional, and oral popular wisdom has also found its way into it. Even the later scribal wisdom of Jesus Sirach cannot get by without this experiential wisdom. The Hebrew term *chokmah* was never narrowed down to education and knowledge; it had a side related to experience and praxis. Among the wise the Israelites also included skilled craftsmen, specialists in ritual (wailing women) and people with much experience of life from whom others took advice.

One constant theme of the whole of ancient literature is that human knowledge is in principle very limited and unreliable. Moreover the biblical texts are not the first to point out that wisdom is corrupted by being associated with wealth and education, though they constantly do so. Already in the teaching of Ptahhotep (2350 BC)[10] there is a warning:

Do not let your heart be puffed up because of your knowledge;
do not be confident because you are a wise man.
The full limits of skill cannot be attained,
and there is no skilled man equipped to his (full) advantage.
Good speech is more hidden than the emerald,
but it may be found with maidservants at the grindstones.

Whereas the deliverance of the city of Abel-beth-maacah by a wise woman is preserved in the earlier narrative tradition of Israel (II Sam. 20.14–22), Koheleth (9.13–16) laments that because of his poverty no one remembered the poor wise man who saved a city from war.

I have also seen this example of wisdom under the sun
and it seemed great to me.
There was a little city with few men in it;
and a great king came against it and besieged it,
building great siegeworks against it.
But there was found in it a poor wise man,
and he by his wisdom delivered the city.
Yet no one remembered that poor man.
But I say that wisdom is better than might,
though the poor man's wisdom is despised,
and his works are not heeded.

Time and again, the imagined, self-satisfied wisdom of the rich and those who claim to be wise is questioned in the wisdom literature in the name of YHWH (Prov. 3.7; 28.11; Job 37.24; cf. also Isa. 5.21).

Be not wise in your own eyes,
fear YHWH and turn away from evil.

True wisdom is granted to little people (Prov. 11.2), but frustrates the devices of the crafty (Job 5.12) so that their wisdom becomes folly (Isa. 44.25),
Wisdom which goes along with distorting justice, lies and despising God is no wisdom (Jer. 8.8f.):

How can you say, 'We are wise and the law of YHWH is with us'? But behold the false pen of the scribes has made it into a lie. The wise men shall be put to shame, they shall be dismayed and taken; lo, they have rejected the word of YHWH, and what wisdom is in them?

Thus time and again fear of YHWH is emphasized as the criterion of true wisdom, a piety which reckons with the mercy and righteousness of God (Jer.9.23).

Thus says YHWH: 'Let not the wise man glory in his wisdom, let not the mighty man glory in his might, let not the rich man glory in his riches; but let him who glories glory in this, that he understands and knows me, that I am YHWH who practises steadfast love, justice and righteousness in the earth; for in these things I delight, says YHWH.'

In the Q tradition Jesus links up to a tradition with elements which are markedly critical of society and rule when he pronounces a beatitude on the uneducated (*nepioi*, Matt. 11.25f. cf. Luke 10.21 and the borrowing from Wisdom 1.21).

> I thank you, Father, Lord of heaven and earth, that you have hidden these things from the wise and understanding and revealed them to the uneducated; yes, Father, for such was your gracious will.

When in I Corinthians, with more or less literal quotation of the Old Testament texts mentioned, Paul builds up the contrast between learned worldly wisdom and the preaching of the folly of the crucified Christ who is divine wisdom, unfortunately we cannot exclude the possibility that he is using precisely this argument to support his own authority and wisdom and to defame the wisdom of Corinthian women.[11] How natural it was for the Christian communities in the first century to recognize the marginalized and poor of their society in the fools and uneducated people of the Old Testament is also evident from the parable of the banquets handed down in the Logia source which picks up the invitation issued by Wisdom in Prov. 9; here it is not those without insight who are brought in from the streets but the (uneducated) poor.

The option for a feminist wisdom theology which begins with the uneducated of the world can and may appeal to early Christian traditions, but in no case may it do so at the expense of Old Testament wisdom generally. Were that to happen, Old Testament wisdom would be being used only as a negative background to the later Christian development. The critique of wisdom has its origins in Israel, just as from the beginning the corruptibility of the prophetic office and the appearance of false prophets is made a theme. The biblical criticism of the wisdom of the wise was not a matter of a prophecy which passed exalted judgments and set itself above all measures, but was in turn formulated by wisdom, including the wisdom of the little people. It is not wisdom itself that is put in question, but a particular kind of self-satisfied, learned (male) wisdom. In the New Testament there are few ideas that are critical of wisdom, but a wealth of positive acceptances of images, ideas and traditions from wisdom. In his parables and discourses the Synoptic Jesus constantly begins from the everyday observation of men and women. He is felt to be a wisdom teacher and understood as a messenger of Sophia, at times even doxologically confessed as God's Wisdom, again closely taking up earlier biblical conceptions of Wisdom. In I Cor. 2.6ff., Paul too takes up the wisdom christology of the hymn-like confessions of faith without any criticism.

IV. Wisdom and fear of God

Angelika Strotmann[12] has addressed as a special problem of the Logia source the words of judgment which are directed against all Israel and could be read as anti-Judaistic. She demonstrates how a closer reading of the Old Testament roots of these words of judgment can prevent such a false reading. In the light of the Old Testament tradition it is hardly surprising that Wisdom in the Q logia often seems to be bound up with ideas of judgment. She appears with threats already in Proverbs (Prov. 1); she calls for a decision, a yes to life, which at the same time is a no to all necrophilia (Prov. 8. 35f.). That may seem shocking, but how could the close connection between wisdom and righteousness be taken seriously if not by a failure to recognize this wisdom or a contempt for it which results in the rejection of her invitation which is given to all? The God of Israel and Jesus is a God of mercy *and* righteousness, a God who makes his sun rise over good and evil but nevertheless destroys the places of the criminals, in the tradition of the sun god Shamash, who is a judge. In this sense even the killing of the present-day messengers of Wisdom will not prevent the judgment. The biblical fear of God has nothing to do with anxiety, but is rather an attitude which reckons with God's effective power in this world and God's uncompromising goodness. If the Old Testament brings out Wisdom as a preacher of judgment and according to Q the Queen of Sheba rises as a witness 'in the judgment with the men of this generation' (Luke 11.31; Matt. 12.31), then these pictures are a challenge to any feminist theology not to offer biblical images of God in the harmless selection made by bourgeois religion.

My remarks support the thesis of Elisabeth Schüssler Fiorenza that feminist wisdom theology must not stop at the femininity of personified Chokmah and the traces of her in New Testament texts. Certainly the feminine talk of God-Christ-Sophia is indispensable for breaking out of the patriarchal ontologizing of theological language and the consolidations of our images of God. But in addition to that, a critical feminist revision and appropriation of the wisdom traditions is called for, which time and again has to do with the question of righteousness and also directs this critically against itself. This reference to righteousness is not only prophetic and not

Silvia Schroer

specifically Christian; it is an essential part of wisdom and the Old
Testament, and beyond that of the ancient Near East – which is reason
enough to encourage respect for ancient religions.

A critical feminist revision of wisdom texts has to discover the function
that they serve for patriarchal society. That function is very evident, for
example, in the book of Jesus Sirach. It must make the female subjects
visible as those who give or receive wise counsel, investigate the wisdom of
Israelite women and their silence, and it must also bring out the remarkable
contrast between a Chokmah with feminine connotations and a process of
tradition which runs through male authorities (Solomon, the father), as it
can be observed in various great religions.[13] The criticism of the 'wisdom of
the wise' is always criticism of the kyriarchy, but the female voice of this
criticism must be made audible in the biblical texts and in our everyday life.
In addition, feminist theology has to venture to transform the ideas current
at that time of a just order to the present day, for example democratic, social
orders, and restore to the centre of theology a concern for creation, the world
of animals and plants, and the everyday life of men and women. Ecofeminist
approaches can also refer back to biblical wisdom in order to demonstrate the
far-reaching connection between injustice in the interpersonal sphere and
the destruction of creation. The advantage of a wisdom theology over a
prophetic theology is that it does not refer to the experiences which a particular individual has of revelation but to something which can universally
be experienced. Wisdom makes use of arguments and plausibilities by
analysing the reality which all can experience and by drawing consequences
for the will of God. Because it can dispense with religious insider language,
it is particularly appropriate for inter-cultural and inter-religious dialogue,
from which too it once came into being.

Translated by John Bowden

Notes

1. For what follows see Silvia Schroer, *Die Weisheit hat ihr Haus gebaut. Studien
zur Gestalt der Sophia in den biblischen Schriften*, Mainz 1996; Elisabeth
Schüssler Fiorenza, *Jesus: Miriam's Child, Sophia's Prophet*, London and New
York 1995; Athalya Brenner and Carole Fontaine (ed), *Wisdom and Psalms. A
Feminist Companion to the Bible (Second Series)*, Sheffield 1998.
2. Christl Maier, *Die 'fremde Frau' in Proverbien 1–9. Eine exegetische and
sozialgeschichtliche Studie*, OBO 144, Freiburg CH and Göttingen 1995. Cf.

Gerlinde Baumann, *Die Weisheitsgestalt in Proverbien 1–9. Traditionsgeschichtliche und theologische Studien*, FAT 16, Tübingen 1996.

3. Angelika Strotmann, 'Weisheitschristologie ohne Antijudaismus? Gedanken zu einem bisher vernachlässigten Aspekt in der Diskussion um die Weisheitschristologie im Neuen Testament' in Luise Schottroff and Marie-Therese Wacker (eds), *Von der Wurzel getragen. Christlich-feministische Exegese in Auseinandersetzung mit Antijudaismus*, Leiden etc. 1996, 153–75.

4. Luise Schottroff, 'The Sayings Source Q' in E.Schüssler Fiorenza (ed), *Searching the Scriptures*, Vol. II, New York and London 1994, 510–34.

5. Dorothee Sölle, 'Zwischen Patriarchat, Antijudaismus und Totalitarismus. Anmerkungen zu einer Christologie in feministisch-theologischer Sicht', *Orientierung* 56, 1992, 130–3.

6. For what follows see the survey on research in Othmar Keel and Silvia Schroer, *'Verdirb es nicht, ein Segen ist darin' (Jes 65,8). Biblische Versuche, die Welt als gelungene Schöpfung zu begreifen* (forthcoming 2000).

7. Hans Heinrich Schmid, *Wesen und Geschichte der Weisheit*, BZAW 101, Berlin 1966, was influential in the German-speaking world; cf. also id., *Gerechtigkeit als Weltordnung. Hintergrund und Geschichte des alttestamentlichen Gerechtigkeitsbegriffs*, Tübingen 1968.

8. Thus very pointedly also Dorothee Sölle, *Lieben und arbeiten. Eine Theologie der Schöpfung*, Stuttgart 1985.

9. Jan Assmann, *Ma'at. Gerechtigkeit und Unsterblichkeit im Alten Ägypten*, Munich 1990; Schroer, *Die Weisheit hat ihr Haus gebaut* (n.1), 12–25; Klaus Koch, 'Saedaq und Ma'at. Konnektive Gerechtigkeit in Israel und Ägypten?' in Jan Assmann et al. (eds), *Gerechtigkeit. Richten und Retten in der abendländischen Tradition und ihren altorientalischen Ursprüngen*, Munich 1998, 37–64.

10. Translation based on J.B.Pritchard, *Ancient Near Eastern Texts relating to the Old Testament*, Princeton ²1955, 412, lines 46–52.

11. Cf. also Antoinette Clark Wire, *The Corinthian Women Prophets. A Reconstruction through Paul's Rhetoric*, Minneapolis 1990, and Elisabeth Schüssler Fiorenza, *Jesus: Miriam's Child* (n.1).

12. See n.3.

13. See Sung-Hee Lee-Linke (ed), *Ein Hauch der Kraft Gottes. Weibliche Weisheit in den Weltreligionen*, Frankfurt am Main 1999.

Jewish Women and the Shekhina

SUSAN STARR SERED

Shekhina: She Who Dwells, She Who is a Neighbour, The Divine Indwelling Presence, The Feminine Aspect of God. Shekhina is a grammatical variant of the Hebrew root – SHIN CAF NUN – meaning dwell, live, abide, presence.

Jewish feminists, like feminists of other faith traditions, have confronted the male orientation and masculine attributes of conventional language and imagery for the Divine. While there are a number of explicitly theological books and essays written by Jewish feminists who address the nature and gender of God,[1] Jewish feminists, for the most part, have tended to focus their attention in the ritual sphere, allowing God language and imagery to emerge as part of the ritual process rather than in a self-consciously theological way. A great deal of the spiritual creativity of Jewish feminists has gone into developing rituals that strengthen community, that sacralize life-cycle events such as weaning or menarche, that comfort the mourning and heal the ailing, and that sacralize freedom and justice – the twin themes of the women's *seders* typically held the week before Passover and that have, over the past two decades, become a feminist institution around the United States. In these and other ritual contexts, Jewish feminists have produced an impressive corpus of songs, prayers, and ceremonies that explore, play with, deconstruct and construct gendered ways of relating to the Divine.

It is difficult to generalize about a new religious movement that is as de-centralized, pluralistic, and eclectic as Jewish feminism, yet I do think it is fair to say that Jewish feminists, for the most part, are more concerned with naming themselves and their ancestors than with naming the Divine. The ritual element that seems to have become the most widespread in Jewish feminist circles is that of beginning ceremonial events with each participant naming herself (in Hebrew, English and/or Yiddish) and speaking out loud the names of female ancestors as far back as she has been able to trace. In this ritual naming, ancestors are invited into the sacred circle, an act that appears to be as compelling to many Jewish feminists as any sort of prayer directed to a higher being, male or female, located outside of the circle. It is usually the case that the loudest 'oohs and aahs' tend to be reserved for those who can name their great-great-great-great-grandmothers, rather than for those who name a female Divine.

In the following section I shall summarize briefly the development of the most prominent Divine feminine image/entity in Jewish culture – the Shekhina. This summary is guilty of gross oversimplification and is not intended to give more than the most preliminary and simplistic sense of traditional Jewish images and notions of the Shekhina. Then I shall illustrate some of the contemporary Jewish feminist ritual understandings of the Shekhina. Afterwards I shall outline reasons why many Jewish feminists are uncomfortable with giving prominence to the Shekhina. Finally, I shall ask if it is possible to think about a feminist liberation and reclamation of the Shekhina.

I. Shekina in early Jewish souces – very brief summary

The Bible contains a few puzzling yet tantalizing references to 'the glory of the Shekhina' and to 'the wings of the Shekhina'. While the meaning of these verses is not at all obvious, the rabbinic sages of the Talmud and Midrash interpreted them as having to do with situations in which the manifestation of God and God's nearness to humankind or to specific individuals is spoken of. Talmudic scholar Ephraim Urbach explains that 'The omnipresence of God-Shekhina is one of the primary postulates (of rabbinic literature). The dicta that speak of the Shekhina do not attempt to describe her, but to explain and reconcile her with the manifestations and presence of God at fixed places and times, whilst avoiding the solution of positing the existence of powers that are separate and emanate from the Lord.'[2] Surveying all passages in rabbinic literature referring to the Shekhina, Urbach concludes that 'the Shekhina is no "hypostasis" and has no separate existence alongside the Deity'. Moreover, 'In the ideology of the Sages of the Talmud and the Midrash the term "Shekhina" is not connected with "Wisdom", and the two are not identified. In all the sayings and stories in which reference is made to the Shekhina, figurative expressions like Princess, Matron (Lady), Queen or Bride are absent. In brief, they contain no feminine element.'[3]

In the course of gradual theological developments that came to fruition in the *Kabbalah* (mystical) literature of the High Middle Ages, the designation

'Shekhina' came to be understood not only as feminine but also as the personification of God's immanent presence in the world. Kabbalistic texts, written by men and prone to extreme objectification of women and femininity,[4] depict a highly esoteric view of creation as a process in which God manifests in a series of emanations. In the terminology of the Kabbalah, God is referred to as *Eyn Sof* (Without End), and is never pictured in human form. In order to create the universe, *Eyn Sof* created ten *Sefirot* (emanations) each corresponding to a different element of his/her divinity. Half of these emanations are portrayed as masculine, half as feminine. The 'lowest' of the emanations, Shekhina, is the aspect of God closest to this world. The Shekhina, a feminine hypostasis of God in Kabbalistic thought, must be re-united with the male Holy One Blessed Be He in order for '*tikkun*' or cosmic reparation to take place.

Esoteric and mystical Kabbalistic writings certainly advanced elaborate philosophical ideas and some liturgical formulations having to do with the gender and the cosmic role of the Shekhina. Yet I believe it is fair to say that for most of Jewish history, for most Jews – male and female – the Shekhina has been relatively insignificant, imbued neither with proto-feminist nor with ritually consequential undertones outside of a few minimal (and, to many Jews, obscure) liturgical formulae.

II. Jewish feminists and Shekhina creativity

With the rise of Jewish feminism in the late 1970s the Shekhina took on new life. Eager to find non-masculine ways to think about God, some Jewish feminists embraced the Shekhina in much the same way that non-Jewish feminists embraced a variety of pre-Christian goddesses. The Shekhina songs and rituals of Jewish feminists have tended to crystallize around two interlinked themes: healing of women's ills and creating of women's communities. Often, these themes are conjoined in songs and rituals of the Festival of the New Moon – Rosh Hodesh, a traditional women's holiday that has enjoyed a renaissance among contemporary Jewish feminists. In part because of the paucity of traditional Rosh Hodesh liturgy and rituals, this festival has been a more fertile ground than the Sabbath or better known holidays for feminist spiritual experimenting. In all-women Rosh Hodesh groups, Jewish feminists have forged communities and spiritual sisterhoods, have explored Jewish sources for hints about the lives of our foremothers, have created novel biblical exegesis, and have searched for spiritual responses to the transitions, triumphs, and life crises that their members have faced over the years.

Shekhina prayers seem to have gathered the most momentum among groups of Jewish women throughout the United States, and more recently around the world, who have been gathering – often in the context of Rosh Hodesh meetings – to help one another find spiritual healing in the aftermath of rape, hysterectomy, miscarriage, and other losses. When the world of male and masculine power has most blatantly failed, perhaps, the need for a feminine Divine becomes most palpable.

While most of the rituals created by these groups remain unrecorded, there are several collections of Jewish women's rituals that can be perused in order to see how Shekhina is given meaning by Jewish women today.

Nancy Helman Shneiderman describes a women's healing ritual that she organized after she had a hysterectomy. I quote here the part of the ceremony that most explicitly related to the Shekhina:

Two holes, about a foot deep, have been dug in the garden before the ceremony. I stand between them holding my womb in a hard pottery bowl to have it blessed and purified by the pouring of water from a pottery pitcher. *I now join both parts of my life together by the planting of my womb. We draw from our depths the essentials of our sustenance. Our spiritual thirst has caused us to look for new ways of cleansing our bodies and souls.*
All say: (While a friend pours water over the womb)
> *Women are like water.*
> *We flow and flow and flow.*
> *Shekhina is like water.*
> *She bubbles from below.*

Nancy: (Transfers womb to greenware bowl for planting)
> *I offer my womb as a covenant, returning it to the earth, honoring the Source of all life. As I plant it in the ground, my mourning is complete and I am released from this part of my life.*

(We planted two pear tree saplings, one over the womb and the other in the empty hole.)[5]

Rabbi Lynn Gottlieb has created and documented a 'Fruits of Creation' ceremony for women who cannot, or who choose not to, give birth. In an anthology entitled *Lifecycles: Jewish Women on Life Passages and Personal*

Milestones,[6] Gottlieb describes a 'Fruits of Creation' ritual held for a woman who experienced early menopause as a result of treatment for breast cancer. The ritual was held on the New Moon, and utilized traditional Jewish symbols such as a prayer shawl and candles. As part of the ritual the women spontaneously formulated a 'litany of grief':

> *Shekhina, She who dwells within all being: I mourn the loss of the child I never bore. I mourn the loss of the mothering I envisioned. I mourn the loss of my ability to bear children. I mourn the loss of...*

We began wailing to a tune Deborah composed until our tears flowed, our hearts were opened, and our spirits felt a release from grief. We filled the (now empty) washing bowl with water and passed it around, washing each other's faces and giving each other a blessing. Then came a calmer, more peaceful listing.

> *Shekhina, She who gives and takes away: I release the feelings of rage I have because I could not birth a child. I release my anger at my husband and forgive him for the times we struggled over our yearning for children. I release my feelings of inadequacy over not being physically able to conceive and forgive myself for difficult times. I release...*

For the last stage of the ritual each participant placed in a bowl a gift or token which expressed some special quality she admired in Deborah.

> *Shekhina, She who eternally creates and renews: I celebrate my devotion to becoming a potter in the face of hardships. I celebrate my ability to grow an abundant garden. I celebrate my relationship with... I celebrate my gratitude for... I celebrate my courage to...*

The women danced in a circle and concluded:

> *Shekhina, we give thanks to you for the ever-present Mystery dwelling within all being, who gives and takes away, who eternally creates and renews life for the good.*

Jewish feminists love to sing – a liberating act in a culture that tradition-ally has silenced women's public voices, and a powerful act of community-building as women's voices mingle and blend in collages of biblical verses and new lyrics written by contemporary women. Several well-known Jewish feminist songwriters have included Shekhina in their lyrics. These writers include Hannah Tiferet Siegel, Debbie Friedman, Matia Angelou, and others. The songwriter who has given the most attention to Shekhina is Geela Rayzel Raphael, a Reconstructionist rabbi whose songs have gained an increasingly wide and active audience in women's groups and synagogues. I have chosen the following three songs that, as far as I can see, present the most elaborate spiritual understanding of Shekhina among contemporary Jewish feminists.[7]

Shechinah, My Sister in the Wind
I feel supported by the universe
From the Source of where all life begins,
Floating through time and space that blankets me
Gently carried by the wind.

Shechinah! Heal my mind and body
Shechinah, I call to you my friend,
Use your powers of radiance
Help my hurting heart to mend.

Your presence in my life so subtly
Sometimes I forget to let you in.
The shelter of Your love protects me
Shechinah, my sister in the wind.

Shechinah, my sister in the wind
I trust Your love to make me whole.
Your Ruach [spirit, wind] rustles in the wind
Your wings cradling my soul.

Shechinah, my sister in the wind
Shechinah, You whisper in the wind
Shechinah, You spiral in the wind
Shechinah, my sister in the wind.
(Geela Rayzel Raphael, 1987)

Shechinah's Web
Waiting for the light to come
and the clouds to shift
The heavens need to open
My spirit needs to lift.
Through times of hope and times of trial
Times of joy and times of change
I hear Shechinah calling me
She's calling out my name.

Chorus :Singin' ah, ah, ah Shechinah (x3)

With all Her mystery, I can't begin to understand
But when I speak to Her
She's always close at hand.
When I search for You, Shechinah
I don't know where to start
But then to my surprise
I find You in my heart. (Chorus)

Gazing through the window, of eternity
Waiting for a sign to come,
its time to turn the key
Invisible blanket of Your warmth
Oh yes, you take me home
My soul finds its comfort
I know I'm not alone. (Chorus)

Women weaving their web of love
Under Shechinah's moon
Candlelight and starry night
is when I hear Your tune
Though nothing's bright as Shechinah's song
When I hear Her voice
I open and ask to receive
and know I have a choice. (Chorus)

At times when I feel lonely
at times when I'm afraid
I find my place within the world
remembering from whom I'm made
Glimmer of light, spark of dew
Overcoming fear

I know that You are with me
I know that You are here. (Chorus)
(Geela Rayzel Raphael, with the help of B'not Ha-Levana, 1988)

Shechinah Coming
Among the many nations, we are a people of peace,
But as the ancient women, we have a longing for release;
Unbinding chains of habit
Painting textured fabric
Brucha Yah [Praise Yah] Shechinah, Arrive!
Chanting sacred stories, her tapestries unfold,
Mysterious, majestic Shechinah our soul;
Dwelling deep within us
Stirring myth within us
Praise be Her spirit, Arrive!

Chorus: Ha-le-lu-ha! Its coming time, we've seen the signs
Coming times we seen the signs,
Shechinah glory will surely shine!

Drawn home to mother, come the exiles dispersed
Reviving holy Hebrew means our cultures rebirth;
Her cloud hovers above
Yerushalayim Her love
Waiting for Her children's return.
Resting in the Temple, she finds a place to alight
Our eagle of protection, Her fire lights the night;
Underneath Her wings
Freilach [happy] voices sing
Yearning for Her Sukkat Shalom. (Chorus)

Raising up our power, the Female Divine
Clarifying vision, the world redefines;
The spark of Her spirit
Calls to those who hear it
Blessed be Her ruach [spirit, wind], Arrive!
Her presence in creation burns bright as the sun,
The moon is Her symbol, darkness undone;
Rosy rainbow flashes
She's rising from the ashes
Brucha Yah Shechinah, Arrive! (Chorus)
(Geela Rayzel Raphael, 1987)

Depicted in each of these songs is an image of the Shekhina as female and associated with such 'feminine' elements as the moon, and an image of the Shekhina as a bringer of comfort – particularly, although not exclusively, to women. In Raphael's songs, Talmudic understandings of the Shekhina's immanence, and Kabbalistic understandings of the Shekhina being that part of God that is closest to humans, is given new theological dimensions. The Shekhina is 'deep within us' and always accessible to us; we simply need to learn how to look and listen.

III. Shekina problems

While rituals and songs such as these are not omnipresent in Jewish feminist contexts, neither are they anomalous – there are dozens if not hundreds of others 'out there' in Jewish feminist communities. Still, as I said earlier, the Shekhina has not caught on to the extent that Jewish feminists may have expected in the first years of their spiritual work. Ellen Umansky has voiced one set of problems that she experiences with Shekhina imagery:

> Were we to identify the Shekhina as Goddess, while continuing to identify the Tetragrammaton as God, we might be accused (with some justification) of moving toward polytheism. While we might counter this by only worshipping the Shekhina, thus retaining the monotheism of our faith, to do so would be no better than worshipping God as Lord. At Rosh Hodesh (the celebration of the New Moon), when I am only with women, it seems right that we call on God as Shekhina, but when I am also with men, it becomes important to broaden my images of God in order to reflect the Divine spark that exists within us both.[8]

Marcia Falk, whose *Book of Blessings* has become liturgical among Jewish feminists, also has rejected Shekhina as a suitable term for Divinity, but for rather different reasons.

> The Shekhina was not originally a female image; it did not become so until Kabbalistic times. And when it became explicitly associated with the female, it did not empower women, especially not in Kabbalistic thought, where male and female were hierarchically polarized . . . In Jewish tradition, the Shekhina has never been on equal footing with the mighty *Kadosh Baruch Hu*, the Holy One Blessed Be He, her creator, her master, her groom, the ultimate reality of which she was only an emanation.[9]

Feminist theologian Rachel Adler quite correctly questions whether it is 'possible to extricate Shekhina from the essentialist (gender) meanings with which it was endowed in Jewish mysticism'.[10] And herein, in my opinion, lies the most critical problem that the Shekhina poses for Jewish feminists. The Shekhina is part of a culture that genders not only aspects of God, but also time (the Sabbath is gendered feminine in Jewish culture), space (Jerusalem is gendered feminine in Jewish culture), and the visible 'heavenly bodies' (the moon is gendered feminine in Jewish culture). It seems to me that the attribution of gender to God, time, and space presents gender as immutably built into the geography of the cosmos. Eternally infused with gender, the universe is understood to be 'naturally' gendered. Human resistance to gender roles, in that case, is both aberrant and futile – the universe itself is imbued with gender.

The problem of the Shekhina raises extremely difficult questions that have to do with the possibility of feminist reclamation of any sort of gendered religious symbol. Can it *ever* be to women's benefit to choose to align themselves with feminine symbols and symbolic objects that are at best objectifications of gender difference, and at worst sacred prescriptions for a hierarchical social order? Isn't it likely to be the case that the reclamation of gendered religious symbols will simply re-animate and re-energize notions of the perpetual gendering of the universe – notions that serve to constrain the possible life paths open to all individuals by making it seem as if socially constructed gender roles are mirrored in – or mirrors of — Divine and cosmic attributes?[11]

IV. Can Shekhina be reclaimed?

There is no doubt in my mind that reclaiming and valorizing the Shekhina is a crucial part of Jewish feminist spirituality. Finding a female Divine voice and a place in the cosmos for female spiritual power empowers women through linking our own lives and identities to a cosmic feminine. Being able to utter the words 'God, She' frees our consciousness in a way that few other acts can – giving us the possibility of conceptualizing a cosmos not ruled by fathers and kings, and there are few verbal experiences that feel quite as good as savouring the feminine Divine roll off the tongue when singing songs of the Shekhina. Yet it is important to bear in mind that gendered deities are two-edged swords, empowering men or women, but also sanctifying gender as the natural order.

At this point in Jewish feminist evolution, while I would not advocate abandoning the Shekhina imagery and rituals that have been created by Jewish feminists, I think it would be wise to begin to think about liberating the Shekhina from the gender identity bequeathed her by her Kabbalistic interpreters. In fact, as we saw in the preceding section, contemporary feminist objections to the Shekhina have tended to centre upon what is seen as Her excessive gendering and *not* upon other aspects of Her meaning. Thus I find it heartening that in pre-Kabbalistic literature the Shekhina did not seem to be female in any culturally significant sense. Rather than personifying a full-blown gender identity curiously congruent with the social roles assigned to human women, the word 'Shekhina' simply expressed a feminine grammatical form – a far lighter (though still not insignificant) cultural load to carry. What was most significant in this earlier period was the Shekhina's immanence, not her gender.

As a Jewish feminist I am honoured to be able to take my theological cue from the pre-eminent Jewish feminist Miriam Simos – Starhawk – who has critiqued Western, patriarchal religious worldviews that situate Deity outside of the world. 'Of course, within each tradition there are exceptions, but in the broad view of Christianity, Judaism, and Islam, God is transcendent, and his laws are absolutes, which can be considered in a context removed both from the reality of human needs and desires and the reality of their actual effects.' The problem, according to Starhawk, is that 'when we believe that what is sacred – and, therefore, most highly valued – is not what we see and sense and experience, we maintain an inherent split in consciousness that allows us to quite comfortably cause pain and suffering in pursuit of an unmanifest good'.[12] Divine immanence, in contrast, imbues all of our actions – to one another and to the very earth we tread – with inherent moral significance.

Jewish feminists like Starhawk invite us to welcome the Shekhina into our world as our neighbour – linked with us and linking us – in complex webs of reciprocal respect and caring, rather than to idealize or reify Her as a female emanation or hypostasis of the transcendent (male) Deity. I find it fitting that Rabbi Akiva, famous for asserting that '"Love your neighbour like yourself" is the greatest commandment in the Torah', is also attributed with teaching that: 'When man and woman are worthy the Shekhina abides in their midst; if they are unworthy fire consumes them' (T.B. Sota 17a). Taking some liberty with Rabbi Akiva's words, I join him in the belief that through acknowledging the worth of both men and women, the Divine Presence is brought into being; lack of such acknowledgment threatens the very survival of our species on this glorious earth.

Notes

1. The most influential has been Judith Plaskow, *Standing Again at Sinai: Judaism from a Feminist Perspective*, San Francisco: Harper & Row 1990.
2. Ephraim E. Urbach, *The Sages: Their Concepts and Beliefs*, Jerusalem: Magnes Press 1979, 47.
3. Op.cit., 63 and 65.
4. For a detailed analysis of gender in Kabbalistic literature see Elliot R. Wolfson, *Circle in the Square*, Albany: State University of New York Press 1995.
5. 'Midlife Covenant: Healing Ritual after Hysterectomy' in *A Ceremonies Sampler: New Rites, Celebrations, and Observances of Jewish Women* ed Elizabeth Resnick Levine, La Jolla, CA: Women's Institute for Continuing Jewish Education 1991, 55–60.
6. Ed Debra Orenstein, Woodstock VT: Jewish Lights Publishing 1994, 40–43.
7. Songs reprinted with permission of the author. Tapes of Raphael's music can be ordered through MIRAJ, 166 E. Levering Mill Road, Suite 240, Bala Cynwyd, PA 19004.
8. '(Re)Imaging the Divine', *Response* 41–42, 119.
9. 'Notes on Composing New Blessings' in *Weaving the Visions: Patterns in Feminist Spirituality* ed Judith Plaskow and Carol P. Christ, San Francisco: Harper & Row 1989, 129–130.
10. *Engendering Judaism: An Inclusive Theology and Ethics*, Philadelphia: Jewish Publication Society 1998, 100.
11. Much of my discomfort with gendered (including feminine) deities is an out-

growth of my fieldwork in Okinawa, the only contemporary society in which women priestesses are the acknowledged leaders of the mainstream religion. The myriad deities that comprise Okinawan religious culture are ungendered or at most vaguely gendered. As I argue in my book *Women of the Sacred Groves: Divine Priestesses of Okinawa* (New York: Oxford University Press 1999), the opposite of cosmic patriarchy is not cosmic matriarchy – Okinawan priestesses do not replace God the Father with Goddess the Mother, but rather acknowledge and pray to egalitarian and loosely or non-gendered cosmic beings.

12. 'Ethics and Justice in Goddess Religion' in *Women's Consciousness, Women's Conscience: A Reader in Feminist Ethics* ed Barbara H. Andolsen, Christine E. Gudorf and Mary D. Pellauer, San Francisco: Harper & Row 1985, 194.

'If We Do Not Love Life': Spirituality and Ethics in the New Millennium

CAROL P. CHRIST

This issue of *Concilium* reflects from different perspectives on a political wisdom spirituality that sustains rather than mutes struggles for survival and liberation. While I agree that survival and liberation are desirable goals, I sense a certain hegemony of discourse that privileges Christian liberation theology and imagines that other discourses are either morally inadequate or can be subsumed under its rubrics.

I am quite aware that there is a great deal of injustice and suffering in our world, and I struggle against its human-created forms on a daily basis. Still, I wonder whether a focus on 'struggle' is an adequate matrix for grounding spirituality and ethics in the New Millennium? Is it yet another way of saying that this earth is a vale of tears? Another way of grounding Christian ethics in an absolute? Or of asserting that Christian ethics is superior to other ethical systems, for example to those that do not *begin* with the notion of struggle?

In *The Ethics of Ambiguity*, Simone de Beauvoir wrote: 'if we do not love life on its own account and through others, it is futile to seek to justify it in any way'. She criticizes ethical systems based on ideological absolutes, including three that she was familiar with: Roman Catholic, fascist, and Marxist. She cautioned that the illusion of moral certainty increases suffering. Those who are certain that their cause is correct inevitably sacrifice the concrete to the ideal. They kill and destroy *without questioning* in the name of a 'higher good' that they believe they understand unambiguously. Against ethical absolutism, de Beauvoir argued for an ethics of ambiguity. As finite individuals and communities we will never have the 'full picture'. Thus we can never know that our decisions and actions are unambiguously 'right'. Humility is a central building block of ethical understanding.

De Beauvoir believed that the struggle to change social and other structures of oppression must be rooted in a prior apprehension of the value of embodied life. If we do not *love life,* there is nothing on which to base our ethics. Life is to be loved 'on its own account' and 'through others'. This grounds love for life in the body and in relationship with other human beings.

I agree with de Beauvoir. In *Rebirth of the Goddess,* I stated that love and beauty are the great gifts of bounteous earth. The Goddess is the intelligent embodied love that is the ground of all being. The ethics of Goddess religion stem from a deep feeling of connection to all people and to all beings in the web of life. We act morally when we live in conscious and responsible awareness of the intrinsic value of each being with whom we share life on earth. When we do so, we embody the love that is the ground of all being.

I. A new song

In gratitude for life and love, I have rewritten a traditional song of praise. This song can be said or sung, silently or aloud throughout the day, on waking, on going to sleep, and at any point in the day one feels grateful – for life and breath, for a beautiful tree, for a bird in the garden, for the presence of a friend, or a child, or a lover, for food to eat – until eventually the whole day becomes a meditation, a prayer of thanksgiving.

> *Praise Her from whom all blessings flow.*
> *Praise Her all creatures here below.*
> *Praise Her above in wings of flight.*
> *Praise Her in darkness and in light.*

This is a new version of the traditional Protestant hymn of thanksgiving or doxology. The original words are:

> *Praise Him from whom all blessings flow.*
> *Praise Him all creatures here below.*
> *Praise Him above ye heavenly host.*
> *Praise Father, Son, and Holy Ghost.*

I have chosen to write new words to this traditional hymn, because, like many others, I have always enjoyed singing it. For me the melody suggests the welling up of thanksgiving from within the body overflowing outwards in community into the expression of praise and thanksgiving. Transforming well-known songs and bringing them into a new context establishes a sense of continuity with the 'best impulses' of inherited traditions and with the 'best impulses' of one's own past self.

This song is sung as part of the offertory portion of the traditional Protestant service, when money is collected from the congregation, to be used for the support of the religious hierarchy and for the missionary and charitable activities of the church. For me, as for many, the placing of money into a basket had little spiritual meaning. But I always loved joining with others in singing the doxology. Changing the context in which the song is sung changes its meaning. I have sung it with women gathered around altars filled with fruits and nuts and seeds in Crete, in front of a flowing spring in Lesvos, and by myself. As I sing, I feel a joyous sense of gratitude for every gift that comes to me in my daily life.

The shift of pronoun from 'Him' to 'Her' gives the prayer new meaning: the locus of divinity is not confined to heaven, but includes both earth and sky. The traditional song evokes an abstract Heavenly Creator who gives blessings in a hierarchy of power relations. The new song suggests that the Source of Life is intimately related to the creatures in a dance of life.

The old song evokes a hierarchical relation between the 'creatures here below', 'the heavenly host', and the Trinity of Divine Power. One imagines a shadowy Father, the Heavenly Creator, who sits on a throne at the top of a hierarchical pyramid, doling out grace and punishment to His underlings according to His inscrutable will. And as Alice Walker's Celie reminds us, we also visualize Him as 'big and old and tall and grey-bearded and white'. The 'creatures here below' are intuitively understood to be 'beneath' Him and subject to His will. The heavenly host, more perfect than the creatures below, occupy a middle rung in the hierarchy.

When offered to 'Her', the song becomes more physical, dynamic, intra-relational. 'She' is intuitively understood to be the Earth and the 'creatures here below' have an intimate connection to Her: they are Her children, born of her body, and part of Her body in the sense that the earth is the body of Goddess. The implication of the traditional song is that the divine power stems from a realm that is not physical and embodied. In the new version, the divine source and the creatures occupy the same sphere, which includes light and darkness, above and below. 'She' is not a distant, ruling, and controlling Other.

The words that replace the Trinitarian formula further a sense of dynamic relation between the Source and the creatures. In the traditional version, the 'creatures here below' passively await the grace of an overlord. But in relation to the parallel phrase 'in wings of flight', one imagines the creatures of earth and sky in constant movement. The Source of Life is not imagined as 'above' and the creatures 'below', because the creatures move gracefully through the upper world, sky, the heavens, as well as on the earth. All creatures are imagined as equally sharing in the grace of life, thus shattering the traditional notion of a hierarchy of power.

The last phrase of the song further overturns traditional dualistic and hierarchical convention. In Indo-European and biblical symbol systems, the light is the realm of divine power, while the dark is the realm of sin, disease, and death. In the new song, the darkness and the light are equally valued as aspects of the realm or body of Goddess. The implication is that the Goddess is with us in good times and bad, in sickness and in health, in death as well as in life.

Understanding darkness and light as two aspects of the same reality undermines a conventional association that undergirds sexist habits of mind. Since Plato, we have learned to see the light as positive, masculine, and mental, the darkness as negative, feminine, and physical. The new song does not stand the traditional dualisms on their heads, validating the darkness and negating the light. Rather it causes us to view them in dynamic relation, like night and day. Implicitly the masculine is affirmed as well as the feminine.

The valuing of darkness and light together also overturns racist habits of mind. Since the entry of the Indo-Europeans into Europe, language and convention have dictated that the 'other' who is conquered is understood as 'dark' in relation to the light-bringing conquerors. In ancient Greece, the old religion was associated with the darkness and death (hence the scholarly designation 'chthonic [earth and underworld] powers'). In recent years, this mentality has been used to foster racism. The 'white' races are said to have brought the 'light' of civilization to a 'dark' continent, whose 'dark' (skinned) people are or were living in ignorance and barbarism. The new song subverts this habit of thinking. To the extent that we understand ourselves as 'white' and 'black', we also see ourselves as equally included in the grace of life. And clearly, the Source of Life cannot be understood only as white-skinned. She is dark like the earth and light like the sky. If anthropomorphic images are used, the Goddess would be both light and dark-skinned.

II. Nine touchstones

Because it is rooted in the ambiguity of life, Goddess religion cannot provide us with a new Ten Commandments or with universal ethical principles. Nonetheless, I have discovered nine 'touchstones' that can help to translate the mythos of Goddess religion into an ethos, a way of ethical living. A 'touchstone' is different from a universal principle or a commandment. Like a beautiful pebble on the shore of the sea, it is discovered by attending to the concrete. It does not derive from a source outside ourselves, but rather is discovered within the web of life. A touchstone can be consulted for guidance, but it does not tell us precisely what to do in any concrete situation. Ethical decision-making is relative to the situations in which we live. New touchstones can be added as they are discovered. Those that have outlived their usefulness can be discarded. The touchstones I have found are applicable to individuals, communities, and societies.

These nine touchstones of the ethics of Goddess religion are: (1) nurture life, (2) walk in love and beauty, (3) trust the knowledge that comes through the body, (4) speak the truth about conflict, pain, and suffering, (5) take only what you need, (6) think about the consequences of your actions for seven generations, (7) approach the taking of life with great restraint, (8) practice great generosity, (9) repair the web.

1. To nurture life is to manifest the power of the Goddess as the nurturer of life. To honour, respect, and support mothers and children. To recognize all people and all beings as connected in the web of life. To embody the intelligent love that is the ground of all being. There are many ways to nurture life: caring for children; tending a garden; healing the sick; creating a hospice for the dying; helping women to gain self-esteem; speaking the truth about violence; replanting forests; working to end war. How different our world would be if we made the nurturing of life the criterion of all that we do. As Arisika Razak stated, 'If we begin with loving care for the young, and extend that to social caring for all people and personal concern for the planet, we would have a different world.' An ethic based on the nurturing of life has a great deal in common with the 'ethic of care' described by psychologist Carol Gilligan as a female mode of ethical thinking. I believe that if men were more involved with the nurturing of life in all its aspects we would recognize the ethic of care as a human mode of moral behaviour.

2. To walk in love and beauty is to appreciate the infinite diversity of all beings in the natural world including ourselves and other human beings and

to sense that everything wants to be loved. When we walk in love and beauty, we open our hearts to the world, to all our relations. We are stunned by beauty and our hearts fill up and spill over with love.

3. To trust the knowledge that comes through the body means to take seriously that our bodies are ourselves and that sensation and feeling are the guardians of life. To experience the joy and pain that come to us through the body. To allow what Audre Lorde called 'the power of the erotic' to lead us to question the denial of pleasure and satisfaction that is inherent in the ethos of domination. To ground ourselves in the earth and to acknowledge our interdependence in the web of life. Trusting body experience also means never to give ourselves over to any authority – no wise man, no guru, no spiritual teacher, no spiritual tradition, no politician, no wise woman, no one. The ethos of domination has encouraged us to trust external authorities. This has led to great suffering and harm. A prayer called the charge of the Goddess says: 'for if that which you seek you find not within yourself, you will never find it without'. Not trusting authorities does not mean that we cannot learn from others. Learning from those who have gone before us is part of interdependent life. But nothing should be accepted unquestioningly. Everything must be tested in our own experience.

4. To speak the truth about conflict, pain and suffering means not to idealize life. Not to deny the realities of our personal and social lives. For many of us childhood and other traumas have been intensified because conflict was denied and we were not allowed to feel our pain. Denial is also a social phenomenon. Americans can continue to assert that they live in the 'greatest society on earth' only if they deny the violence and ecological destruction that is occurring all around them. Many in Hitler's Germany apparently denied the reality of the gas chambers. Denial is only possible when we sever our minds from our bodies. When we trust the knowledge that comes through our bodies we feel our own joy and suffering and the suffering and joy of others and the earth body.

5. Taking only what you need and thinking about the consequences of your actions for seven generations are touchstones that come from the Native Americans. The first acknowledges that conflict – taking the lives of other beings – is inherent in human life, and thus encourages restraint.

6. The second affirms interconnection and asks us to consider not only our own needs, but the needs of all our relations for seven generations as we take and give back to the circle of life. Seven generations is a very long time. It is about as backward and forward as the human imagination can stretch.

We are not asked to hold ourselves to impossible models of perfection, but to consider the consequences of our actions on a scale we can comprehend.

7. Approaching the taking of life with great restraint is implicit in taking only what we need. I have made it a separate touchstone because those of us who live in industrialized countries take so much more than we really need without thinking of the lives that are lost. And because as individuals, communities, and societies we so readily resort to violence and warfare to resolve personal, ethnic, and national conflicts.

8. The 'spirit of great generosity' advocated by Dhyani Ywahoo is an important guide as we work to transform our cultures and societies. Generosity begins with ourselves. If we are to gain the power to act, we must acknowledge that no single one of us can take on all the burdens of the world. As we recognize our strengths and forgive our limitations, we can begin to approach others with a generous spirit. Ywahoo urges us to 'speak the best of one another and perceive the best in everything', recognizing that 'it is a strenuous discipline in these times to practise this'. Yet it requires great discipline to understand the harm that Europeans have done to Native Americans and other people of colour, without concluding that 'Europeans are bad' and 'European culture has nothing of value in it'. Or to acknowledge the evils of sexism without deciding that 'all men and everything they have ever done is bad'. Or to learn of the roles of Christianity and Judaism in the suppression of Goddess religion and the ethos of interdependence without coming to believe that 'Judaism and Christianity express no positive ethical values'. Or to see the threat that national conflicts present to the human race and the web of life without stating that 'all of our political leaders are evil'. Though great harm has been done, very few people or groups have nothing to commend them. When we polarize situations, we make it difficult for our 'adversaries' to change, not to mention that we begin to perceive ourselves unrealistically as 'all good'.

9. The last touchstone, repair the web, reminds us that we are living in a world where the bonds of relationship and community are broken by violence. Stemming from the Jewish commandment to 'repair the world', this touchstone calls us to transform our personal relationships, our social and cultural institutions, and our relation to the natural world. In our time the nurturers of life must work to establish greater harmony, justice, and peace for all beings on earth.

These nine touchstones define the ethos of Goddess religion, providing a framework for ethical decision-making but not a blueprint for action. There are still hard decisions which we must make as individuals, communities, and societies. These must always be made with a sense of humility as we take responsibility for the ambiguity of all moral judgment.

The Spirituality of Our Ancestors

CLARA LUZ AJO LÁZARO

The sound of drums was heard, issuing an invitation to the party. The old house belonging to the devotee* Tomasa Nenínguez in the district of Pueblo Nuevo in the city of Matanzas was filling up with people who gradually crowded together in the main room of the house. Everything there was in movement, far more so than at the sort of party that could happen at any time and for any reason in Cuban houses. This was a special party, it was a party called 'saint's party' or 'saint's touch', a liturgical celebration observed by the faithful of the religion of Santeria.

I. A process of synthesis and selection

This religious observance, African in origin, is one of the most popular in Cuba today. It developed during the years of the slave trade, when numerous African ethnic groups were brought to the island. Among these were the Yoruba, or Lucumi, as they are called in Cuba, who brought one of the strongest, most established and developed cultures of Africa, with a stratified and diversified cosmological vision of the world and the cult of the *orishas*. They came above all from south-western Nigeria, from the Yoruba-speaking Oyó, Ijesá, Egbado tribes, and from Ghana and Togo, from Ekití, Ewe, Fon and others.

The Santeria religion, a basic part of the piety of the Cuban people, is the product of a process by which the Lucumi, brought from Africa and enslaved on Cuban soil, tried to preserve their own ideas and traditions disguised under elements of the Christianity imposed on them. They translated what they heard from the whites into their own concepts, taking the

---

* *Santería*, described here, has no English equivalent for many of its terms. It literally means devotion to the saints. Its practitioners are *santeros* (male) and *santeras* (female), for whom the term devotee is here used of both. It invokes spirits, here left as *orishas* (Trans.).

greatest possible advantage of their situation as 'Christians' to improve their conditions while continuing to adore their own divinities.

This was how they came to give names to their gods, using Catholicism as a façade behind which to celebrate their own rituals under the pretext of honouring Catholic saints. They did not reject these saints but brought them into their own vision, became used to them, transformed them, humanized them in their own likeness, and so in this way protected their divinities.

The course the slaves followed was not moving from their own gods and goddesses to the Christian God, but the reverse process, taking the God of the Christians and, above all, their saints to where their African deities resided. Guiding themselves simply by the similarities they found between their *orishas* and the catholic saints, they gradually fused their deities with the hagiology of the church. Furthermore, living together with people from other ethnic groups produced an admixture of other beliefs and in the end meant that the Yorubas' religious system had to go through a process of synthesis and selection. The *orishas* who resisted this process began to be redefined and basically associated with the saints and virgins of Catholic devotion.

As a result of this religious process, the *orisha* was called (in Spanish) *el santo* 'the saint', this form of religious expression was called *santería* (literally 'saintery') and its initiated followers *santeros* and *santeras* (literally 'sainters'). Santeria became a Cuban product, transforming the African elements proper to its origins, keeping some of them and creating new ones.

At that 'saint's party' in the devotee Tomasa's house, all these elements were being expressed in a flurry of movement, bodies, rhythms, dances and songs. The magic of ritual symbols and gestures was taking hold.

II. A relationship of interdependence

In the middle of the big colonial-style room, the believers had formed a circle and were dancing to the rhythm of three sacred drums. These drums, called *bata* drums, are important liturgical elements that Santeria inherited from the Yoruba tradition. Of all the countries of America, Cuba alone has managed to preserve this authentically Yoruba tradition, and even today these drums have kept the same form as the original model, examples of which can still be found in various regions of Africa, still with the same shape and name. At that moment in the room, these drums were speaking their rhythmic language, calling on the divinities.

In the circle, the devotees of both sexes were dancing. The circle is the symbol of their own conception of the world and existence, since devotees believe that the world, the earth, our physical universe, the place where the lives of all beings that inhabit it, is the *áiyé*, and we humans are the *ará-áiyé*, that is, the people who inhabit the world. There is also a parallel world to our real world, the *órun*, in which all persons, animals, trees, nations, cities and so on have their spiritual and abstract double. Conversely, everything that exists in the *órun* also exists in material form in the *áiyé*. It is in the *órun* that our gods, the *orishas*, live, who are the *ará-órun* or inhabitants of the *órun*.

The *órun* is made up of nine planes or spaces situated one above the other. Four of these planes are below the earth, one of them, the middle one, coincides with the space occupied by the earth, and the other four are above it. It is significant that *órun* and *áiyé* thus make up a common whole. The *órun* enfolds the earth, framing it above and below, so making up the totality of the world. This means that the earth is the material, concrete level of the world and at the same time represents the concrete, materialized aspect of the *órun*. Heaven and earth are two inseparable aspects of the *áiyé*, and so the *áiyé* and the *órun* are also two inseparable levels of existence.

This unity is symbolized by a pumpkin made up of two halves put together, the lower half representing the earth, the *áiyé*, and the upper half representing the *órun*. Inside the pumpkin is a series of elements, including human beings and the gods. In other words, the space of the *órun* encloses and at the same time includes the whole space of the *áiyé*, including the earth and the heavens, and as a result all the supernatural bodies associated with air, land, and the waters are invoked and arise from the earth.

There is an interdependence between the whole universe and nature, community, family, and individuals. They are the two halves of the pumpkin, which make up the world. Nothing can happen in isolation from other things; everything has to be in relationship in order to exist, to have value. The whole cosmos and individuals are interrelated, everything is integrated, and it is this relationship that gives meaning to life. Everything has meaning because it is related to other things and other people, to the whole community. Individuals on their own have no value, but they have value in the community: the community is what gives value and meaning to their lives. The world and persons are part of a single body, a single pumpkin. Nature and all the beings that live in her, including persons, live in a relationship of interdependence. All need everything and everyone else.

In the ritual wheel formed that afternoon by the dancing devotees, this relationship of interdependence was shown by the music, the dance, the chants, the body movements of those who were dancing, all forming a whole, a whole through which the *orishas* were invoked. These divinities show the characteristics of the human personality and of our Cuban national character in a particular way, but at the same time, through them, this tradition sacralizes the body, nature, human relationships, and the whole of life in a constant interaction between the sacred and everything.

The Yoruba tradition does not go in for theological and philosophical statements about the supreme god. Oloddumare, for believers of the Yoruba tradition, is simply beyond the reach of human understanding. This God creates the *orishas* so that these divinities can be those who govern the world, and it to them that men and women pay ritual homage and address their requests, while Oloddumare remains distant and set apart, indifferent to human problems.

III. Vital energy

In Cuba, in Santeria, the name of this supreme God is Olofin Olorun Oloddumare, each one of these names representing functions and powers acting in the world.

Olofin is the creative power that made the *orishas*, the world, the animals, and human beings, 'the cause of and reason for all things'.[1]

Olorun represents another of the energies or powers that form life on earth, the sun, heat, light, the vital energy essential to everything that forms part of the life of earth.

Oloddumare represents the universal law, the entire universe, the laws of nature, the whole of existence. When I asked the *babalawo* ('father of the mystery') José Arondo, known as Changó Laddé, the Chief Devotee of the city of Matanzas, about this, he immediately bent down and touched the ground with his fingertips: 'There are no words to describe Oloddumare, daughter; he is the greatest, everything, but he lives elsewhere, nobody thinks about him: those who have to do with us are the *orishas*, the saints are the ones who live with us.' The writer Natalia Bolivar has a very interesting passage referring to Oloddumare: 'He is in all our actions, in the wisdom of Olofin, in the goodness of all the *orishas*, and in Echu, because good and bad also form a whole in Oloddumare . . . For the Yorubas the world is a gourd whose lower half is the earth and upper half heaven. This means that inside the gourd is everything – Oloddumare.'[2]

So each one of the names of the supreme god of Santeria represents one of the powers or principles that regulate existence. One notable aspect is that the description believers in Santeria give of Olofin Olorun Oloddumare transcends a masculine image. Devotees speak of Olofin as sun, life, of Oloddumare as something that cannot be described in words, the laws of the universe, and so on. These definitions show that the idea of God is closely related to manifestations of powers that rule the universe and the earth, and although the personage who appears in myths and legends representing the supreme God is masculine, the relationship devotees establish between their divinities and the forces of nature helps them to depersonalize the divinities.

So in the Yoruba tradition and consequently in Santeria, the supreme God is not an object of adoration and worship. The powerful divinities called *orishas* are the ones who govern the world, and each of these has been endowed with one of the powers of this distant God. 'Each *orisha* becomes an archetype of activity, of profession, of function, one complementing another and all representing the totality of the powers that rule the world.'[3] Pierre Verger describes this relationship between *orishas* and their sons and daughters who provide an image of these divinities as 'pure power, the immaterial *axé* that becomes perceptible to human beings only when the *orisha* is embodied in one of them. This person chosen or possessed by the *orisha* is called its *elégùn*, and is the person who has the privilege of being "mounted" by it. He or she becomes the vehicle that allows the *orisha* to return to earth to greet and to receive tokens of respect from its descendants who evoked it.'[4] (In both the *áiyé* and the *órun* there are three principles or powers: *iwá*, *axé* (or *aché* in Spanish), and *àbá*. These powers make possible and regulate all existence in the universe. *Iwá* is the power that allows existence in general; it is linked to the air, the atmosphere, and to breathing. *Axé* is the power of fulfillment, which dynamizes existence and allows it to come about. It is the energy that underlies everything and guarantees individual existence. *Àbá* is the power that gives purpose and direction; it accompanies *àxé*. Existence unfurls in this web of powers and principles, in a continual quest for balance among the elements.)

The *orishas* are bearers of *axé*, the underlying energy, and each of them represents a force of nature, such as the waters of the sea, the fresh water of rivers, fire, wind, harmony and peace, the strength of metals, and so on. It is very important for believers to receive *axé*, to accumulate it, sustain it, and re-create it through rituals and direct contact with the divinity, trying to incorporate everything that goes to make up the *áiyé* and the *órun*:

'Receiving *axé* means incorporating the symbolic elements that represent the vital principles, essential to everything that exists, in a particular combination that individualizes and confers a definite meaning.'[5]

At the same time, significantly, each *orisha* represents the archetype of a different personality, and the Yoruba pantheon of divinities is so wide that it contains representations of virtually all the more general archetypes of the human personality. So among these divinities can be found the naughty child; the coquettish and sensual woman; the virile, *macho*, woman-chasing man; the strong, warrior woman; the more patient and benevolent woman; the wise woman; the pure woman seeking perfection; the protective mother; the wise old man; the young man full of vitality, or strong and warrior-like, or independent, or masochistic, and so on. Each son or daughter of an *orisha* can recognize the components of his or her own personality in his or her *orisha*. And not only character traits: physical features of bodily build, looks, health, defects, and also sexual characteristics such as vitality, potency, fecundity, frigidity, and so on all come from their *orisha*. 'Examining initiates, grouping them by *orishas*, one notes that they generally possess common features, both in their biotype and in their psychological make-up. Their bodies tend to bear, to a greater or lesser extent, depending on the individual, the sign of the mental and psychological powers that inspire them.'[6]

These divinities have a completely anthropomorphic character: they are not perfect; they are divinities who have all the human faults and virtues. They present a mixture of good and evil, which in the Yoruba vision are two inseparable aspects of existence. That is to say: good/evil dualism has no place either in Santeria's outlook on life or in its divinities.

So Santeria – unlike other forms of religious expression, which require their followers to adopt a certain approach, behave properly, and possess certain good qualities if they are to become like their divinities – accepts its devotees straightaway into the community of believers exactly as they are, since all of them have an *orisha* father or mother who shares the same faults and virtues. This is why the transgressions and weaknesses of any believer are accepted with understanding in the community and are tolerated by people who recognize the character of the divinity him- or herself in such behaviour.

So in this form of religion the concept of sin as disobedience against one's God does not exist. People should try to act well, but if by inclination or by their own nature they do something wrong, something that harms the community or an individual or society in general, they will reap the consequences of their wrongdoing, but not as punishment. Furthermore, if they are good sons or daughters of their *orishas*, they will keep up a strong identification with their divinity and gradually the personality of the *orisha* will become stronger and stronger in each person, bringing out both its own virtues and its own faults in that person.

IV. They live with us

These divinities are not all-knowing, omni-present, and all-powerful. This is very much part of the anthropomorphic quality of *orishas* mentioned above. When I asked *babalawo* Changó Laddé about this, he told me, 'Daughter, in other religions the gods are above people; in our religion the gods are on earth: they live with us and are like us. They are not perfect because they form part of human life, which is not perfect. Perfection does not exist, my daughter, and so the *orishas* don't know everything, and can't do everything or be everywhere at the same time. They are like us.' Which means that human beings are accepted with their contradictions, their problems, their joys and sorrows, their faults and virtues – their real lives, in effect.

And on that festive afternoon at the devotee Tomasa's house, the dance with its accompanying songs and movement had reached the stage when the energies of nature are summoned to make themselves present so as to restore the old balance between them and people.

Each *orisha* has its own rhythm, its chants, its dance movements, its colours, its symbols, its ritual clothes. The rhythms were accompanied by the voice of the singer, whose voice also directs the antiphonal choral music proper to Santeria. This whole musical ensemble invoked and summoned the *orishas* of both sexes who would become present in the bodies of their sons and daughters through 'possession trance'. (It is the power of *axé* that allows *orishas* to manifest themselves in persons through the experience of trance or possession. This is a psychological state in which the person concerned, prepared for this through the initiation ritual, exteriorizes an archetype of behaviour that is generally repressed by circumstances, culture, social traditions, and so on. This behaviour, which forms part of the person's own archetype, always corresponds to the behaviour that characterizes his or her *orisha*.)

The rhythm of the *batá* was very infectious, and gradually the house filled with people. Everyone was dancing: it was truly a feast of the body, a total movement bringing together people of different races and both sexes in one and the same liturgical expression. Little by little, through the trances their sons and daughters went into, the divinities became present: the first to arrive was Elaguá, the child god who opens and closes the courses of fate. He always comes first of all, and it is he who carries messages to the *orishas*. Then came two female *orishas*, Ochun, goddess of love and sensuality, mistress of the fresh waters of earth; and Yemaya, mistress of the seas and mother of life. They were followed by Ogun, master of metals, and then by others.

At one point during the party, these divinities, embodied in their sons and daughters through trance, walked about the house, greeting and blessing the people there, embracing them, handing on their energies, talking to them and giving them advice and solutions to their problems. The divinities danced with the people and ate with them, spoke to their sons and daughters and then, at a moment determined by them, were helped to return to their normal state. It was a celebration of the sacred, made present in bodies, in embraces, in the energy of life and nature shared in community.

Translated by Paul Burns

Notes

1. N. Bolívar Aróstegui, *Los Orishas en Cuba*, Havana 1994, 86.
2. Ibid.
3. P. Verger, *Orixás*, São Paulo 1981, 21.
4. Ibid., 19
5. J. Elbein dos Santos, *Os Nagó e a Morte*, Petrópolis 1993, 42.
6. G. Cossard-Binon, 'Contribution à l'étude des candomblés au Brésil: Le candomblé angola' (Doctorat de troisième cycle, mimeo), Paris 1970, 215.

Brigit: Soulsmith for the New Millennium

MARY T. CONDREN

The nuns went to Mass. The circle-dancers danced. A yoga group was in full session in the corner. A tree-hugging group swayed around the trees. Chanters wafted Indian music in the distance. Some just went to breakfast.

The amorphous group and the texture of that morning in the West of Ireland testified to the far-reaching changes in the landscape of Irish religion and spirituality. These women – Catholic, post-Catholic, Protestant, pagan – met to celebrate, excavate, and liberate the traditions and legends surrounding the spirit of Brigit.

For the past hundred and fifty years, clerical and religious abuse, the betrayal of innocence, a dead hand of colonizing clericalism, and wars fought ostensibly over religion, have paralysed the Irish religious imagination. But against this backdrop, the figure of Brigit – metaphor, muse, goddess, saint and keeper of the flame – emerges today to re-kindle Irishwomen's spirit.

For the past seven years, we in the Institute for Feminism and Religion[1] have taken various aspects of the traditions surrounding Brigit and woven them into a festival celebrating her feast-day: 1 February, the first day of spring in the Celtic calendar. The journey has just begun; our questions have barely been asked.

This year the quest took us to Belfast. One hundred and thirty women from all traditions and none gathered to explore the spirit of Brigit through music, crafts, poetry, artwork, dance, and reflection: peace workers, community activists, artists, poets, psychotherapists, teachers, full-time parents, musicians, and theologians. All returned at the end of the weekend to their homes in Ireland and abroad: renewed, refreshed, energized.

The darkness of winter was over: a new spring had arrived. Hope had triumphed over despair; life over death. Brigit's daughters, *Keepers of the Flame*, committed themselves to nurturing the seeds of her fire for the coming year.

I. Why Brigit?

But one might be entitled to ask: Why Brigit? Why does her spirit still inspire today's Irish poets, artists, musicians, and soul seekers? What might the traditions of Brigit have to offer to contemporary women's search? In this article I will attempt to sketch out some of the possibilities and point towards some of the implications.

Although in the Roman tradition Brigit is known primarily as a fourth or fifth-century saint, and foundress of a monastery at Kildare, the spirit of Brigit reaches back much further than that. By taking over shrines, churches, and mythological sites, the figure of Brigit has effectively incorporated many aspects of the wisdom literature of ancient Ireland. [2]

Today, we draw on her pre-Christian roots, the archaeo-mythology of her sites, her Christian *Lives,* and the rites to be found even in contemporary folklore, to bring women together in search of new cauldrons to hold, ferment, and nourish our hungry spirits. Against the backdrop of marching bands, violent oppositions, and the patriarchal mythologies crucifying Irish cultural and political life for the past thirty years, Brigit's spirit is fresh, untainted, and multivalent.

Lighting candles, we explain – tongue-in-cheek – that these are *pre-Reformation candles.* The old dichotomies collapse under the weight of laughter; the old orthodoxies strain to the sounds of music; the old dogmas sway in the dancing of freed spirits.

But this is not to say that the spirit of Brigit is ungrounded. The female spirit of Old Europe personified, her healing shrines are found in the most remote places. In European history, her sons, *Brigantia* – the last defenders of old Europe – fought off the colonizing efforts of the Romans.

Given her European background, the newly emerging Christian church needed to negotiate with her. Brigit is said to have acted as Mary's midwife in giving birth to Jesus. Moreover, according to popular culture, she saved their lives. When Herod's men sought to slaughter the Innocents, Brigit (drawing on ancient Lupercalia imagery) ran through the streets to distract them, allowing Mary to escape.

In Irish folklore, when Mary was too embarrassed to submit to the rite of churching Brigit again came to her rescue. She took a rake, inverted its prongs, stuck candles in each one and placed it on her head. Preceding Mary into the church, she drew the congregation's attention away from her friend, allowing Mary to enter without shame or embarrassment. In return for such great friendship, Mary is said to have granted Brigit a feast day ahead of her own Feast of the Purification, 2 February. In reality, 1 February was too deeply rooted in popular rite and tradition to be amenable to the Gelasian policy of converting ancient pagan festivals to those of the church.[3]

Brigit's ambivalent status and her rootedness in the rites, artefacts, and rituals of the Celtic soil ensured that her stories and legends have been passed down from generation to generation; her relegation to folk-culture, that her rites have remained relatively free of clerical intervention; her female gender (she can't be taken seriously), that she escaped the efforts to colonize the female spirit. Her multivalency now ensures that meditating, reflecting and theorizing on her images, symbols, stories, and rites can once again inspire, encourage, and nurture the emerging struggle towards integrity of women today.

In the *Lives* of Brigit, mythological and saga themes constantly emerge and are indistinguishable from her legends. At her birth, her mother had one foot inside the door and the other outside, bridging the world of pagan and Christian. Her mother was a slave; her father, a free and rich man. She forms a perfect bridge or threshold between the worlds of pagan and Christian, rich and poor, women and men. Brigit in her saintly aspect constantly eludes the attempts of hagiographers to tame, colonize, or neutralize her.

Among her many characteristics, Brigit was patronness of healing, poetry and smithwork. For the millennium year in Belfast, our theme was 'Brigit as Soulsmith'. In the words of poet Anne Kelly, we invoked her:

You who turned back the streams of war
whose name invoked stilled monsters in the seas
whose cross remains a resplendent, golden sparking flame
come again from the dark bog
and forge us anew.[4]

II. Old Irish mythology

The blacksmith, the traditional figure of alchemy, magic, and culture, was a feared and revered figure in most traditional societies and Indo-European mythology.[5] He transformed nature to culture, forged the instruments of agriculture, shod the animals and often maintained the village fire. As we will see when we turn to the sources, there is much more to Brigit and the blacksmith than originally meets the eye: Brigit's smithwork proves to be quite unique.

In old Irish mythology, in *The Book of Invasions*, we find evidence that the figure of the blacksmith was distinctly problematic.[6] The king of the *Tuatha Dé Danaan* (People of the Goddess Danu), King Nuadu, lost his arm in battle. Because he was now physically blemished, Nuadu had to resign from the kingship. His resignation made way for Bres, of the Fomorian race (one of the invaders), who was granted the kingship provided he treated the people well. However, Bres began to levy heavy taxes on the people and they groaned under the weight of the oppression.

In the meantime, Dian Cecht, blacksmith of the Tuatha Dé Danaan, had made Nuadu an arm of silver, but he was still technically blemished and the arm had begun to fester. But Dian Cecht had a son, Miach and a daughter, Airmid, both doctors. Going to Nuadu, they actually *grew* another arm for Nuadu, using the words, *sinew to sinew, and nerve to nerve be joined.* Nuadu was able to resume the kingship and dethrone the oppressive powers. But they had reckoned without Dian Cecht. Profoundly jealous of his son's achievement, Dian Cecht attempted to kill Miach. Three times he wounded him seriously, but on each occasion, Miach was able to heal himself. On the fourth and final attempt, Dian Cecht succeeded.

Airmid was grievously distressed at what had happened and went to her brother's grave. On Miach's grave, 365 types of herb were growing: one for every day of the year, for every nerve in the body, and every human ailment. She began to gather the herbs, arranging them carefully on her cloak, systemizing their properties. Dian Cecht, incensed at the powers of his son and daughter, irretrievably scattered the herbs. The legend ends that had it not been for the jealousy of Dian Cecht, the blacksmith, we might have lived forever with medicines to cure all ills.

The story clearly reverses some mythological themes. Death enters the world, not through Eve's sin or Pandora's chaos, but through the jealousy of the blacksmith father. Like Antigone, Airmid attempted to honour her brother's memory, but was caught up in patriarchal jealousy and rivalry. Already, therefore, the figure of the blacksmith is problematic. Miach and his sister, Airmid, drew, not on the transformative power of metal, but the transformative powers of life to bring about their healing. The culturally constructed silver arm cannot compete with the power of life itself. The rejection of their arts would have far-reaching consequences.

The ambivalence of the blacksmith recurs in another tale, *The Battle of*

Moytura.[7] Irish legend tells of many invasions, but the invaders were always made welcome, provided they respected the ways of the Irish and honoured their goddesses. For instance, they were allowed to come to Ireland provided they honoured the ways of the goddess by giving the goddesses' names to the land. Marriage and syncretism traditionally enabled the Irish to tolerate diversity, to welcome the stranger.

In *The Battle of Moytura* things began to take an ominous turn. Goibniú was the smith of the People of the Goddess Danú, but the weapons he made were magical. Brigit was a member of the *Tuatha Dé Danaan* and in order to cement relations between two distinct peoples, she married one of the invaders, Bres of the *Fomorians*.

Goibniú made a weapon for Brigit's son, Ruadán, who thanked him by turning the weapon on him and attempting to kill him. Goibniú survived the triple attack but then turned the weapon on Ruadán, killing him. On hearing of the death of her son, Brigit shrieked and wailed. According to the text: 'this was the first time shrieking and wailing was heard in Ireland'. The *Battle of Moytura* ends with an ominous intonation from the Goddess, Morrigú, signalling the end of matri-centred Ireland:

Peace up to heaven,
Heaven down to earth,
Earth under heaven,
Strength in every one.

I shall not see a world that will be dear to me
Summer without flowers,
Kine will be without milk,
Women without modesty,
Men without valour,
Captures without a king . . .
Woods without mast,
Sea without produce . . .
Wrong judgments of old men,
False precedents of lawyers,
Every man a betrayer,
Every boy a reaver.
Son will enter his father's bed,
Father will enter his son's bed,

Every one will be his brother's brother-in-law . . .
An evil time!
Son will deceive his father,
Daughter will deceive her mother. [8]

III. Lives of Brigit

Clearly the culture of weapons, made possible by the arts of the blacksmith, is distinctly problematic: the spirituality of the old pre-Celtic matri-centred Ireland was antithetical to the new spirit now being introduced. In the Christian *Lives* of Brigit, this theme continues.

In one version of her *Life*, Brigit had a bishop, Conlaed, who was particularly fond of fine vestments. Brigit gave these vestments away to lepers, beggars, or to whomsoever she felt needed them more. Several times she had to make the clothing reappear to appease Conlaed's wrath. A crisis arose when he appeared one day in search of them, and all she had to offer was a 'garment like to the skin of a seal's head'. Exasperated, Conlaed set out for Rome for the third time, presumably to get more vestments, but Brigit said to him: 'You will not get there and you will not come back. And so it was fulfilled, for wolves devoured him.' [9] Possibly it was in relation to this and other incidents that a famous refrain of the early Celtic church was composed:

To go to Rome, much labour, little profit
The King whom thou seekest here,
unless thou bring him with thee, thou findest him not.
Much folly, much frenzy, much loss of sense, much madness (is it), since going to death is certain, to be under the displeasure of Mary's Son. [10]

In another version of this story, however, Conlaed is not a bishop but a smith. The garments of the religious officiaries of old Europe, the 'garment like to a sealskin', referred to the power to be found by returning to the womb, symbol of the source of life itself. We know that in the old Indo-European tradition officiating priests curled up in such garments during their rites. [11] The seal was a symbol of immortality, but equally, the sealskin garment simulated the womb. In other rituals (possibly later) kings bathed in the blood of the slain mare, or entered menstrual huts at specific boundaried times to immerse themselves in female entropy. [12]

The old European priests entering the sealskin garment, the cave of Newgrange, or Loch Derg were returning to the womb of the earth for rebirth and regeneration. Even the early Christian churches remembered this: figures known as *sheela-na-gigs* were often placed on the door lintels. Foetal-like in appearance, they held their genitals apart signifying to the person coming in that they were re-entering the womb/church, a place where our origins were honoured and remembered. The church was a place of peace: weapons must be left aside; the power of life and death remained the prerogative of divinity.[13]

This anecdote by the early church historian, Bede, is telling in this respect:

When the Chief Priest of the British, Coifi, had heard the message of Christianity (CE 627) he, together with the king, renounced his faith and set about destroying the temples and altars that he himself had previously dedicated. And so Bede relates, 'He formally renounced his empty superstitions and asked the king to give him arms and a stallion – for hitherto it had not been lawful for the Chief Priest to carry arms or to ride anything but a mare – and thus equipped, he set out to destroy the idols.'[14]

In the culture of the blacksmith, social prestige has resided not in the ability to enhance and co-operate with the life-force and the earth, but in the military ability to effect victory, develop weapons, and dominance based on grandiosity.

Whether smith or bishop, Conlaed represented the emerging culture where nature was not enhanced but superseded. The bishop, Conlaed's, fine vestments were outer garments of grandiosity, pretension, and power. Holiness and awe was not naturally encountered in the artefacts of nature, but socially, culturally, and artificially induced by the ostentatious garments of religious culture.

It goes without saying that only privileged members of the privileged sex could wear such garments. Moreover, such new religious officiaries would have to free themselves of all the symbols of abjection, that is to say all reminders of origins: menstrual blood, milk, contact with women. Not accidentally, the twelfth-century Synod of Cashel forbade the Irish to baptize their children in milk – one of the last symbolic remnants of matrilinearity.[15]

A clear set of oppositions appears to be emerging. The first is the cultural transformation represented by the blacksmith: the culture of rivalry, ostentation, war, destruction and death. The other is the transformation found when entering the womb/earth/cave or other representation of birth and re-birth, the transformation made possible by contact with the sources of life itself. The fires of the blacksmith apparently turn nature into culture, but what kind of culture and at what cost?

IV. The culture of the blacksmith

The problem may well be related to the profound cultural changes induced by the manufacture and culture of weaponry that the blacksmith made possible. Scholars as diverse as Marija Gimbutas, René Girard, and Riane Eisler have argued that profound cultural changes were brought about with the introduction of weaponry.

Girard points out that while animals fight, they seldom fight to the death. However, the human development of projectiles and missiles short circuits the instinctive brakes to mimetic crisis found in animals. Therefore, he argues, the rise of weapons and the ability of humans to use projectiles in their battles is what finally distinguishes humans from animals. [16]

Patriarchy has thrived on developing and maintaining various dualisms: heaven/earth, sacred/profane, male/female, culture/nature, pure/impure. Such dualisms and logical oppositions are now clearly exposed as predicates of power relations. Nevertheless, they continue to grip unsuspecting imaginations in their power. This culture was sacrificially achieved by the profound cultural splitting at the heart of the last two thousand years of patriarchal development. As I have argued elsewhere, such sacrificial practices and theologies are lethal in their consequences.[17]

At the turn of this century, against the sacrificial fires of the First World War then burning throughout Europe, a young Irishman, James Joyce, set out, self-consciously in his own words: 'to encounter for the millionth time the reality of experience and to forge in the smithy of my soul the uncreated conscience of my race'. [18] At a time when the boundaries of Europe were being re-drawn, Joyce's definitive gesture embodied Nietzsche's critique:

> But blood is the worst witness of truth; blood poisons and transforms the purest teaching to delusion and hatred of the heart. And if someone goes through fire for his teaching – what does that prove? Truly, it is more when one's own teaching comes out of one's own burning! [19]

Joyce's craft was exile; his anvil, loneliness, and his gesture broke defini-
tively with the security of his upbringing. One of the first post-modernists,
his intellectual and moral courage inspired a whole new generation of
intellectuals to break with the sacrificially oppositions and their political and
religious counterparts.

Today, Irishwomen are perhaps being asked to go further: to encounter
again the transforming powers of Brigit, our Soulsmith for the new millennium.

V. The fire that does not burn

Brigit as patroness of smithcraft had transformative powers that lay in a very
different kind of fire than that used by the blacksmith. Fine vestments and
military weapons both signified a culture of power, dominance and elitism.
Brigit used very different weapons. At times of battle, like the Morrigan, she
used *magic mojo*, psychic warfare, rather than weapons to confuse the opposing sides.[20] She put them to sleep and gave them sweet dreams of victory
without harming anyone; she placed clouds between opposing sides in battle
so they could not see one another. At one of her major sites, the Curragh in
Kildare (the Church of the Oak), no weapons were allowed to touch her
sacred oak tree. Not only did Brigit give vestments away, but she also gave
her father's sword away to a passing beggar.

The smith fires of Brigit are also quite different. In her church at Kildare
in the fire-temple (it can be seen to this day), her nuns tended the fire for
twenty days. On the twenty-first, they left it to Brigit to tend it herself. [21]
Like the Vestal Virgins of ancient Rome, whose dedication and purity of
intention safeguarded the integrity of the political order, Brigit's nuns were
charged symbolically and actually with maintaining the fires, the symbolic
heart (hearth?) of the state.

Fire was also the means through which Brigit knew if her nuns had been
faithful. Every morning, one of her nuns, Darlughdacha (the Daughter of
Lugh) went to collect the seed of the fire. On one unfortunate morning,
when she returned, the fire had burned through her apron, symbolizing that
her purity had been compromised. Shamefully, she confessed to Brigit that
indeed a blacksmith had admired her ankles. [22] Brigit told her to put coals in
her shoes to purify herself once again, and Darlughdacha eventually became
her successor at Kildare.[23] The stories bear evidence of an old purification
fire ritual, but the importance for us is that Brigit's followers were charged

with holding the *seed of the fire* on behalf of the community. The *fire would not burn* providing they remained focussed, and undistracted by flattery.

Like her counterpart, Sul/Minerva, in her fires at Bath, the fires of Brigit *did not burn*. This theme emerges clearly in her *Lives*. When she was born, the surrounding people saw pillars of fire shoot from her house, but were amazed that the house was intact. At her ordination as bishop (another story!) a fiery column shot from her head and was seen for miles around. Brigit was known as the *Fiery Arrow*.[24]

In an old *Genealogy of Brigit* those who invoke her protection chant the following words:

> I shall not be slain,
> I shall not be wounded,
> I shall not be prisoned,
> I shall not be gashed,
> I shall not be torn asunder,
> I shall not be plundered,
> I shall not be downtrodden,
> I shall not be stripped,
> I shall not be rent in two,
> Nor will Christ let me be forgotten.
>
> Nor sun shall burn me,
> Nor fire shall burn me,
> Nor beam shall burn me,
> Nor moon shall burn me.[25]

For Irishwomen today our questions are these: What kind of fire does not burn? How do we keep Brigit's flame alive? How can we guard and protect the seed of the fire? These were the questions we wrestled with in Belfast at Brigit's festival. In the space here, I can only make hints and suggestions for our future journeys.

As a nun in the prophetic tradition Brigit took mercy as her distinct virtue. Her transforming powers, her smithwork, are allied to those of healing and poetry. Her fire is the fire that burns within, the life-force infused at birth into each one of us.

Her festival traditions recognized as much. On the morning of Brigit's day, traditionally women took a seed of the fire, put it in a sock, and went out to pound the earth. They were waking the *gnéart* (life-force), reminding the cold winter earth that spring had come. Their song was significant:

> Today is the Day of Bride,
> The serpent shall come from the hole.
> I will not molest the serpent,
> Nor will the serpent molest me.[26]

On 1 February the serpent, the symbol of regeneration, was said to come out of the depths and was referred to as the noble queen. As part of the festival, an effigy of the serpent was pounded.[27]

On Brigit's Eve, women placed her cloak outside the house. Through the night, the spirit of Brigit was said to pass over blessing the cloak with her spirit. In the morning, the women took the dew soaked cloak back in, cut it up into little pieces and used the pieces to cure the sick – animals, pregnant women, and even delicate birds. At one of our festivals, a woman told how her grandmother used the *brat* (the cloak) to wrap sick birds which she then placed in the ample folds of her breast for warmth. Her 'chirping granny' came alive again through her memories.

Brigit may be patroness of smithcraft, but her anvil was that of the soul; her alchemy, that of the spirit; her *fire that does not burn*, the life-force within. Attentive to our soul-work, we keep the life-force ablaze and focussed on the work of justice and mercy.

Conclusion

This exploration has barely scraped the surface of the rich traditions surrounding Brigit, or even her patronage of smithwork. Many other aspects can be explored and in our future festivals we will continue to gather together under her cloak diverse groups of women committed to soul-work.

At the festival in Belfast, in our final gathering, we forged our spiritual weapons for the year ahead, drawing on her symbols. We invoked the protection of her dew-soaked cloak; we cleansed ourselves with water from her wells; we drank milk from the pure white cow; we dipped her bread in the honey of her bees to nourish us for the journey ahead.

In a nuclear world, the old images no longer serve us. Our attitude towards the earth, our bodies and our souls must change. Our repudiation of the earth and our origins in women's bodies must give way to a profound sense of gratitude and responsibility.[28] From the sacrificial fires of patriarchy, we must shift toward the burning fires within. From the burning fires of the Inquisitions, we must now turn towards authentic sources of empowerment by committing ourselves once again to becoming daughters of Brigit: *Keepers of the Flame.*

Notes

1. For details of the Institute, consult our website: http://www.anu.ie/ifr.
2. Extensive bibliographical details on Brigit can be found in my book *The Serpent and the Goddess: Women, Religion and Power in Celtic Ireland*, San Francisco: Harper and Row 1989.
3. Extensive records of the folklore surrounding Brigit are to be found in the Folklore Department of University College Dublin.
4. Unpublished poem
5. See Ivan Mazarov, 'The Blacksmith as "King" in the Necropolis of Varna' in *From the realm of the ancestors: an anthology in Honor of Marija Bimbutas* ed Joan Marler, Manchester CT: Knowledge, Ideas and Trends 1997, 175–87.
6. Cf. *Lebor Gabála Eireann* ed R. A. S. MacAlister, 5 pts, Dublin: Irish Texts Society, nos. 34, 35, 39, 41, 44, 1938–56.
7. Cf. *Cath Maige Tuired* ed Elisabeth A. Gray, Dublin: Irish Texts Society 1983.
8. 'Second Battle of Moytura' in *Ancient Irish tales* ed T. P. Cross and C. H. Slover, New York: Barnes and Noble 1969, 48.
9. *Thesaurus Paleohibernicus: A Collection of Old-Irish Glosses, Scholia, Prose and Verse* ed Wh. Stokes and John Strachan, 2 vols, London: Cambridge University Press 1903, vol. 2, 347. For different versions of this story, see *Bethu Brigte* ed Donncha Ó hAodha, Dublin: Institute for Advanced Studies 1978, 34,64.
10. These words, found in *Codex Boernerianus*, were written by Sedulius. They are thought to be linked with Brigit and are partially echoed in words in the Appendix of *Bethu Brigte*. However, there they refer to Brigit's craftsman, Condla. Cf. *Bethu Brigte*, 34–64.
11. Cf. W. Warde Fowler, *Roman Festivals of the Period of the Republic*, New York: Macmillan 1899, 311.
12. Masao Yamaguchi, 'Towards a Poetics of the Scapegoat' in *Violence and Truth: On the Work of René Girard* ed Paul Dumouchel, Stanford, CA: Stanford University Press 1988, 187. In the Irish context, there was up to the twelfth century, at least, a ceremony, recorded by the traveller, Giraldus Cambrensis, when the king bathed in the blood of the horse/Goddess.Cf. *Gerald of Wales: The History and Topography of Ireland* ed John J. O'Meara, Harmondsworth: Penguin Books 1982, 110.
13. Cf. James H. Dunn, 'Síle-na-Gcíoch', *Eire-Ireland* vol. 12 (1977), 68–85.

14. Bede, *Historia Ecclesiastica Gentis Anglorum: A History of the English Church and People*, trans. Leo Sherley-Price, Harmondsworth: Penguin Books 1974, 127–28.

15. *Gesta Regis Henrici Secundi Benedicti Abbatis* edited from Cotton Mss. by Wm. Stubbs, London 1868, 1:28.

16. René Girard, *Things Hidden Since the Foundation of the World*. Research undertaken in collaboration with Jean-Michel Oughourlian and Guy Lefort, trans. Stephen Bann (Books II and III) and Michel Metteer (Book I), London: Athlone Press 1987, with revisions to the English edition. Originally published as *Des Choses cachees depuis la fondation du monde*, Editions Graset et Fasquelle, Paris 1978.

17. Mary Condren, 'The Role of Sacrifice in the Construction of a Gendered Social Order and Gendered System of Representation', unpublished doctoral thesis, Harvard University 1994.

18. James Joyce, *Portrait of the Artist as a Young Man*, Harmondsworth: Penguin Books 1968, 252–53.

19. Friedrich Nietzsche, *Der Antichrist* trans. R. J. Hollingdale as *The Anti-Christ* (1895), Harmondsworth: Penguin Books 1971, 171.

20. The term is Barbara Mor's, Cf. 'The Morrigain', *Woman of Power*, No.15, Winter 1989–90, 60.

21. Cf. *Gerald of Wales: The History and Topography of Ireland* ed John J. O'Meara, Harmondsworth: Penguin Books 1982, 88.

22. Cf. R. A. S. MacAlister, 'The Fire Walk in Ancient Ireland', *Man* 63 (1919), 117–118; J. Mair, 'Darlughdacha – Eine Vergessene Heilige', *Frigisinga* 5, No. 34 (1928), 433–35.

23. For full bibliographical references to these stories see *The Serpent and the Goddess*.

24. *Three Irish Glossaries* ed. Wh. Stokes, London: Williams and Norgate 1862, xxxiii- xxxiv.

25. *Carmina Gadelica* ed Alexander Carmichael, 2 vols, Edinburgh: Constable 1900, 169–72.

26. Op.cit.,169.

27. Op.cit.,170. It is possible that this could either be a reference to the whipping with the *februum* which formed part of the Lupercalia celebrations, cf. Warde-Fowler, *Roman Festivals*, 311, 320.

28. Cf. Margaret Miles, *Practicing Christianity: Critical perspectives for an Embodied Spirituality*, New York: Crossroad 1988.

In the Movement of Wisdom: Wisdom Rituals and Liturgies as Spiritual Resources in the Struggle for Justice

SILVIA REGINA DE LIMA SILVA

Feminist spirituality has nourished and inspired women's organizations and groups in their rediscovery of their own identity and spirituality and in their commitment to the struggle for life. By feminist spirituality I understand the creative and novel forms in which we women have re-interpreted the experiences of God in our lives. Liturgies have become a special setting for putting this spirituality into effect.

Our liturgies are as diverse as we women are ourselves. But in the tapestry we weave from our diversity, we find common threads or similar shades, tones of sorrow or rebelliousness, expressions of indignation but also of a firm hope. This way of facing up to life produces a different way of celebrating.

This reflection sets out to share certain elements that characterize liturgy and celebration based on feminist spirituality. They are elements recovered from different liturgical celebrations, engraved above all on my memory and in my heart. Together they form an approach to the movements and rhythms, the tastes and fragrances of Wisdom. So may she lead me.

I. Wisdom out in the open

Women have shown a great deal of wisdom in deconstructing the patriarchal world from below and from within, seeking to re-name the major experiences of life on the basis of their own practice. This means turning their backs on a life confiscated by patriarchalism and becoming co-creators of a new humanity. Liturgy is one of the spaces that is being redeemed and given new meaning by women. There is no overt concern with recovering the traditional liturgical space, though this too is being transformed in some respects. But it can certainly be said that women, together with other groups involved in the struggle for life, have discovered and recovered liturgy as an expression of their love for and commitment to the God of life, the God who strengthens their liberative endeavour.

This liturgy re-named by women has a new *locus*. It is an invitation to come out from the space traditionally understood as sacred to meet Wisdom out in the open, in the streets and squares, in mass demonstrations, in family celebrations, in daily life. This new setting brings a new understanding of liturgy. In this way, different instances of celebrating faith in the God of life, of spiritual strengthening on the personal and the community level, of affirmation and renewal of our commitment to justice and human dignity, can all be see as liturgy.

II. Liturgy and symbols

Women have shared this new space and liturgical understanding with other groups and communities, as I have said. In Latin America these include Afro-Latin Americans (of both genders), workers in agriculture and industry, base communities, indigenous women, young people, children and others who are still capable of believing, of celebrating their dreams and of daring to put them into action. These joint liturgies are people's celebrations with a rich and deep symbolic language.

They include a great variety of symbols created out of actual situations, which have gradually become consecrated through their very use and repetition. Among these, nature's presence is felt as a companion and witness. The flowers so often offered – red, white or yellow – tell stories, symbolize lives. They are the symbol of so many lives 'disappeared' under military regimes, but they are also, through their torn-off petals, a cry from women abused in the silence of their homes. The earth that indigenous and peasant women bring speaks against its concentration in the hands of absentee landowners and of its desire to be fertilized so as to feed the poor. Barefooted, black women and men sing their lament of protest against their permanent exile from their lands and culture. Candles light up the dark nights that have taken and still take so many women and men victims of repressive systems, of a false democracy that silences dissident voices. The candles are joined by the cross, another symbol of the martyrs eliminated in the struggle for justice. A Bible wrapped in chains cries out against a religion that has justified and legitimized massacre and slavery and is still an accomplice in discrimination, sexism, and racism.

These symbols speak of a macro-social reality and give fresh strength to daily relationships. They are all woven together by Wisdom, who watches over daily life. Bread, empty pots, rice, beans or *tortillas*, and children's games are also brought in as liturgical symbols. They all speak of life in its richness of diversity and forms of expression, so I could go on describing them for a long time . . .

III. Liturgy: a space for rebuilding life

As we have seen, our liturgy stems from our daily lives; it invokes and celebrates the presence of Wisdom in our struggle as companions for justice. The life offered in liturgical celebration is actual life, with its mixture of joys, sufferings, struggles and dreams. In this way, liturgy becomes an occasion for looking at life as it is offered to us, for accepting its limitations and contradictions. It is a special occasion for being in harmony with life and with the Wisdom made manifest in it. This search for harmony and meaning makes liturgy a space for rebuilding one's life.

The celebrations bring out rites, moments and symbols that make it possible to celebrate personal and community sorrows, to exorcize guilt, and to commemorate the little/great achievements of daily life. Water, fire, embraces, long silences, a word of consolation – all make possible the experience of reconciliation with oneself, the recovery of faith in the goodness of life, and the renewal of commitment in the struggle for justice.

Liturgical celebration thus becomes a space where women can draw strength to rebuild their lives on the basis of their decision to *be* – a *being* formerly denied and now beginning anew as subject, as daughter, sister, comrade. The transformation undergone on a personal level works through into the community. The community is challenged to change, to experience new relationships showing greater respect for life and human dignity.

IV. Liturgy as subversive memory

Gathered around a brazier, women recount their stories, break their former silence and recover their strength, the light that rushes in through their words.[1] The liturgy that rebuilds and fortifies life possesses a historical dimension, one of memory. Celebrating struggles for conditions worthy of life and dreams of liberation means celebrating the memory of those, women and men, who have believed and celebrated their faith in the God of justice who walks with people, heals, and liberates.

In this way, the communion women experience from liturgy starts from the most immediate situation but extends to embrace their ancestors, who are remembered with affection. In these celebrations we name prophetic women great and small, simple women living everyday lives, sanctified by their daring to think beyond what was permitted them. Women who died of loneliness, others who were victims of violence, overt or concealed: their blood cries out for justice; their screams echo in the silences of a society that still murders. These women were a living and transforming presence in history; when their names are called out, we all answer, 'Present', as we believe that those who have gone from this life committed to the struggle for justice carry on their liberating commitment through our bodies and communities and walk with us in love.

V. Liturgy as festival and utopia

Liturgy is memory and also festival. Festivals are part of the lives of all peoples. In the midst of life's contradictions, in the midst of adversities and uncertainties, we find room to hold a festival. Festivals are moments of truce in the battle of life. They are a parenthesis opened in everyday life in which to experience the deep taste of joy, of meeting, so that back in everyday life we can identify and be grateful for the little pleasures that life has to offer. Our liturgy takes on this festive dimension.

Liturgies, like festivals, celebrate life, rekindle hope, and anticipate dreams. They are a special time in which the impossible becomes possible and utopias find their *topos* in reality. In festivals, as in liturgy, we touch the heavens, we touch our dreams with our fingertips and for a few minutes experience the delight of life lived in freedom and love.

Liturgy as festival is an anticipation of the enjoyment of the fullness of life – fullness hidden and negated by unjust and oppressive relationships. Liturgy is an anticipation of what we believe in, of the world of justice and equality that has still not come into being. This makes it possible to renew our hopes, recover our strength, and fill ourselves with energy for the challenges we face daily. Liturgy is an occasion for stroking our dreams so that desolation and despair do not take over our hearts.

The festive dimension of liturgies provides occasions for nourishing ourselves, for sharing our bread, for feeding one another. These moments re-create the deep meaning of eating together, which is present in various religious traditions. The loaded table has become a characteristic of celebrations among the people. The little each person brings to the table is multiplied and also becomes a symbol of the divine abundance and fullness.

In celebrations the meal, besides being a symbol of communion, is also an expression of the desire to move forward, to regain one's strength and not get left by the wayside. Music and dancing complete the setting of a festival. Women and all the different groups that are struggling for justice feel themselves liberated, re-appropriate their bodies, and express this in movements of their bodies, which become sensitive to the presence of Wisdom, listen to her, smell her, feel her closeness, allow themselves to be guided and moved by her.

VI. Liturgy and recuperation of the body

The body is the place in which we experience the world. For feminists, the body has ceased to be an individual category and become a social category with political dimensions. Social injustices, the sufferings brought about by the sins of racism, sexism, and classism are a denial of the dignity of bodies. Liberation projects are rooted in everyone's own body.

One challenge facing women is this re-appropriation of their own bodies. Becoming conscious of one's corporeality is key to any integral liberation.[2] This new awareness contributes to moving beyond the dualist concept by which even struggles for vindication were related to the body. Liberation discourse also theorized about the body, favouring certain macro-social aspects to the detriment of others related to everyday life and the quest for happiness.

In liturgical experiences, bodies are present in their material, actual dimension. Liturgy recovers the importance of the body as a place of salvation, and in liturgy we celebrate the awareness and joy of being body, body that is good from its origin in creation. The closeness of Wisdom brings the body back as a house we live in and in which the Divinity also dwells.

In our celebrations we recall the accounts of healing related in the Gospels, in which being healed represented a break with the limited space in which the body moves, opening it out to new spaces and possibilities of life.[3] In our rituals we learn to listen to and enter into communion with the body in all its completeness. These are therapeutic moments at which we can release suffocated cries, silenced words, and unexpressed desires and so take steps toward liberation and recovery of health.

These rituals teach us to love our own bodies. We become aware that we are body together with other bodies, and that the healthiness of my body brings life and health to others. Recognizing one's own body's beauty and loving it as the work of divine creation, the house in which Wisdom dwells, is an invitation to love, cherish, and care for the bodies of others. And this becomes a way of recuperating the healthiness, goodness, and beauty of the universe.

VII. Feminist liturgy – expression of a holistic faith

Feminist spirituality discovers life itself as the setting for manifesting God. Divine Wisdom is wrapped up in the everyday, in the struggles to transform relationships of domination and violence into ones of reciprocity and respect. By entering into the realm of the Spirit, of Wisdom, we find that she moves beyond interpersonal relationships and those between the human creature and God. We discover the whole universe as a common setting for meeting and communing.

This holistic dimension of spirituality is present in liturgy. This has meant a learning process for Christianity, which, by focussing its worship and celebration on revelation based on the Word of God, has not taken creation adequately into account as the setting of revelation and, therefore, the liturgical space *par excellence*. Through our ancestral religions, we are learning to recognize and celebrate the presence of the cosmos in our liturgy. We are earth, made of earth, with the smell and colour of earth; earth is our origin and our destiny – and also our task as long as we walk on it. This task is to preserve it, to care for it as we do for our own house, and to strive to make it truly a home for everyone.

This cosmic dimension of our liturgies takes many forms. As an example, here is part of one feminist liturgy, a celebration of the Last Supper, in which communion with the universe is experienced and its four elements – earth, fire, water, air – evoked, as are the four seasons of the year and the four cardinal points of the compass. We address each of these (as they affect Costa Rica) in our celebration:

. . . the south, from where the cold and wind of winter come. Thanks be to this season, in which everything rests and sleeps, to be newly reborn in spring; thanks be to the wind that buffets us with its force and caresses us with its gentle breeze.

. . . the east, from where the dawn of each day comes. Thanks be to spring, the season that renews everything – earth, plants, animals, ourselves. Thanks be to earth, from which everything springs and to which everything returns. We remember that we are *mapu-che*, people of earth.

. . . the north, from where the heat of summer comes to embrace us after days and nights of cold. Thanks be to the season of shining sun, refreshing nights and full moons. Thanks be to fire, the eternal spark of life.

. . . the west, from where evening comes. Thanks be to the autumn, season of fullness, of abundance, of maturity. We give thanks for water, the element that cleanses and refreshes us, for rain, seas, lakes, and springs. We are water, we are earth, we are air, we are fire. We give thanks for what we are.[4]

A holistic celebration views diversity as a principle of creation. Diversity is both riches and challenge at the same time. To travel together, considering, respecting, and celebrating differences, has been a long and difficult journey, a permanent apprenticeship. Based on the principle of diversity, there can be no justifiable superiority or inferiority. 'We are simply cosmic, earthlings, beings of the cosmos and of the earth, who need one another and exist only on the basis of a common existence on the basis of the interdependence of our differences.'[5]

VIII. In the lap of Wisdom

Finally, a word about the place or community in which feminist liturgical celebration takes place. I have found it in various places and enjoyed it in various forms.

The main thing is to keep the community of women as the reference. The framework of the community is the sense of love and care for one's own life and the lives of others. It is a community with different criteria for membership, no longer those of religious denomination or even the ecumenism traditionally embraced by the Christian churches. There is something more: the feeling of sisterhood. The Wisdom that dwells in us calls us together and awakens a deep sense of being sisters in us. We feel we are sisters, we commit ourselves to each other's lives, we care for one another – no matter in what part of the world, though it is better when we are close and can come together and celebrate more often.

Together we heal our wounds, share our lives, laugh, retell stories, anoint ourselves with oil and perfumes, strengthen each other. 'This sisterhood discovers ways of making fun of the powerful and the violent, of denouncing the emptiness of their pretensions, of being capable of laughing at their arguments . . .' It is still 'the sisterhood of the catacombs, of prisons, of concentration camps, of witches, of poets'.[6] But it also continually needs to become more visible and better respected in its right to gather and celebrate. It is an inclusive community that invites all to its different meeting-places, in houses, at corners, in open spaces. All who approach will be welcome, always provided that they are motivated by a sincere passion for life in each and every one of its forms and creatures, and always provided that they are willing to commit themselves to the search for justice and happiness.

Conclusion

Liturgy in the form I have described, besides celebrating and nourishing the struggle for justice, broadens its significance. It discovers a new mysticism that, although it may appear less combative, in fact involves the whole of our being.[7] We immerse ourselves in the celebration to the point where this is no longer something external to us but 'part of our own personal experience, of our communion with all forms of life, with all the cosmic energies'.[8] Liturgy refreshes us and gives us new heart, it makes us remember that love, responsibility for others, care, and tenderness are all words to be recalled in our demonstrations and protests. Liturgy invites us, in the midst of our struggles, to create a space for grace; our festival makes us capable of allowing ourselves to be drawn along and enveloped by the currents of Wisdom.

Translated by Paul Burns

Notes

1. See Mary Judith Rees, 'Rito: Santa Cena reciclada' in *Con-spirando*, No.13, Santiago de Chile, September 1995, 44–46.
2. V. Martínez and D. Muñoz, 'Re-descubriendo el cuerpo: nuevas energías para el cambio' in *Con-spirando*, No.12, Santiago de Chile, June 1995, 9–11.
3. U. Seibert-Cuadra, 'La salvación se hace cuerpo: mujer y sanación en los Evangelios' in *Con-spirando*, No.12, Santiago de Chile, June 1995, 45.

4. Rees, art. cit., 44–46.
5. I. Gebara, *Teología a ritmo de mujer*, Madrid 1995, 139.
6. Rees, art.cit.,15.
7. Martínez and Muñoz, art.cit., 11.
8. Gebara, op. cit., 144.

Conclusion: Towards a New World in the Power of Wisdom

MARÍA PILAR AQUINO

The articles that make up the body of this issue come from different ethnic, racial, cultural and geographical sources. The viewpoints that inform each of them derive from different intellectual, religious, ecclesial, theological and academic traditions. The Table of Contents of this volume is a good indicator of the varied nature of the subjects and of the areas of concern and fields of action of the writers. Nevertheless, this plurality of places, viewpoints and writers has a principle of coherence running through all the contributions included here. In effect, the basic principle that makes this volume possible and gives it unity is our experience and understanding of the Power of Wisdom. This principle provides the platform from which we examine the feminist spiritualities of struggle in the various contexts in which we live.

The content of the articles reflects the growing development of a new theological feminist language, which expresses our perceptions of Divine Wisdom from our struggles to bring about justice, well-being, equality and human dignity in all parts of the world. As the various articles show, we all share the conviction that these struggles are inspired and maintained by a feminist spirituality lived in the Power of Wisdom. This spirituality has roots in the daily round of people's lives, emerges in differing global contexts, and expresses itself in culturally plural forms. So this volume of *Concilium* departs from monocultural visions and traditions of spirituality to open the way for critical feminist visions and spiritualities seeking expression in an intercultural language.

The consistent development of feminist spiritualities of Wisdom over the past few decades is neither accidental nor incidental. In my view, there are three main reasons to support this assertion. The first derives from the noticeable tendency for socio-political and religious movements to re-articulate their strategies for change and to insert themselves into new spheres of influence on both local and global levels. These movements have strengthened their commitment to confront and eliminate the kyriarchal[1] systemic domination characteristic of the current paradigm of global free-market capitalism as well as its dehumanizing effects, clearly visible in the spread of injustice, inequality, and social exclusion. The agenda of these movements is devised by numerous women and men intent on generating a new social power with the ability to move history towards new situations of authentic justice, political equality, and socio-ecclesial inclusion. The struggles waged by these movements show that the excluded social groups are forming new convictions, visions and languages in their search for trans-formation into a new world order.

The second reason derives from the visible tendency of these movements to connect their struggles with critical religious traditions supporting and working for objectives of liberation. These objectives can be summed up, for example, in the rich feminist notions of justice, equality, well-being, human dignity, freedom, and fullness of life. For feminist movements around the world, the religious traditions of critical Wisdom are those that provide backing for their struggles to achieve the objectives of liberation. Divine Wisdom, as Elisabeth Schüssler Fiorenza says, does not dwell in kyriarchal institutions or in text but 'among the people',[2] in the quests and struggles for liberation in the midst of a world in which suffering caused by injustice, poverty, inequality, and social insecurity abounds.

The third reason derives simply from the absolute inability of kyriarchal religions to provide a meaningful spirituality to support the struggles of these movements. In effect, kyriarchal religious institutions have for many years demonstrated their virtually complete blindness to the powerful presence of Divine Wisdom dwelling in people, but they are totally blind to the dwelling of this divine presence in global feminist movements and struggles. This inability and blindness are still leading the 'priests of the kyriachy' to spread and multiply a spirituality of oppression, the only effect of which is to help in the spiritual genocide of the entire human race.

For these three reasons, I believe that the feminist spiritualities of Wisdom are creatively demonstrating the possibilities of the present historical situation to engender a new world.

The work of those who carry the message of Divine Wisdom to the world comes up against a global context in which the élites in control of kyriarchal power daily generate endless avalanches of 'spiritual' messages. The aim of these messages is to confer unquestionable certitude and absolute certainty on the present model of global free-market capitalism. These messages serve – often with great success and coherence – to present the global market as the sure source of happiness, well-being, security, and feelings of trans-cendence. The global market comes across as the highest authority in the reasonable ordering of people's lives, as what gives direction, meaning, and value to their existence. The main dogmatic principles presiding over this model are economic efficiency, open competition, and individual gratifica-tion.

For the kyriarchal élites, the global market is the new religion, that which guarantees sustainable human development and in which they carry out the 'priestly functions' of maintenance and celebration, promoting a spirituality that proclaims true democracy, egalitarian electronic communication, and voluntary participation in the life of the global market. The powerful reli-gious and spiritual component of this model produces an inverted reality that prevents people from seeing the effects of the global market, such as widespread poverty, massive exclusion, systemic inequality, and 'women's bodies consumed by patriarchal discipline'.[3] These effects, rather than diminishing, are in constant growth all over the world.

It is in reality the spirituality of this model that has the effect of producing mechanisms in people's minds that prevent them from believing that the model can be fallible, reversible, or changeable. The contents of this spirituality, as Schüssler Fiorenza points out, 'foster a quiet resignation and create political paralysis that concerns itself with little beyond individual survival'.[4] Such is the power of the spirituality of the neo-capitalist global market that even many feminist movements do not dare to examine it critically, still less dissent from it. For this reason, the view held by many people (women as well as men), that there is today a 'crisis of spirituality', is neither opportune, nor correct, nor adequate, let alone honest. The truth is that the spirituality of the present kyriarchal model is stronger than ever. There is in fact no such crisis because, as Franz Hinkelammert has indicated, 'one single paradigm has imposed itself in an unquestionable manner . . . [and this] victorious paradigm acts in the name of the most absolute certainty'.[5] What we are seeing today is that kyriarchal globalization promotes an abstract universalist spirituality, which supports the concentra-tion of kyriarchal power in the priestly élites of societies and religions and also works to suppress critical traditions, plural identities, and alternative projects.

In this context, the work of those who have accepted Divine Wisdom includes three tasks: (1) to stand up to the homogenizing avalanche of kyriarchal spirituality through strengthening critical feminist spiritualities; (2) to dismantle the spiritual mechanisms that support the false determinism of kyriarchal systems through strengthening feminist visions of transformation of society; (3) to support and motivate the various endeavours to counter élitist kyriarchal globalization through strengthening the many feminist struggles taking place throughout the world.

If the twentieth century has rightly been called 'the women's century',[6] the twenty-first needs and cries out for struggles to bring about a situation we might call 'the century of critical feminism'. The articulation of a critical feminist language in which to express our experiences, understandings, and visions of spirituality has a central importance in this project. There is no doubt that the different traditions of critical Wisdom that have played their part and still do so in our varied contexts of religion and culture constitute a prime source, flowing into both the formation of this language and the contribution we can make to transforming global kyriarchal powers. In this sense, the various approaches to Divine Wisdom made in this volume of *Concilium* all share the assertion that Divine Wisdom creates and sustains a just order of human relationships founded fundamentally on justice. Divine Wisdom fosters humanity and enfolds it in compassion, mercy, love and hope. The power of wisdom is to set free, to set up spaces in daily life in which well-being, true joy, humanizing emotion, liberating understanding, and celebration can be experienced by all.

The presence of Divine Wisdom, because it excludes oppressive and dehumanizing relationships, fosters and supports a world in which life is worth living.[7] Divine Wisdom sees the spiritualities, actions, and attitudes of the kyriarchal élites as deserving of condemnation for dominating and exploiting humankind and the environment. So, for critical Wisdom, justice is the foundation of understanding, discernment, and the practice of an ethical way of life that can be considered right, honest, reasonable, and just. In these traditions, Divine Wisdom not only deliberately appears within social groups suffering under and resisting injustices but also empowers them to struggle against these injustices for liberation and its objectives. This is why we have sought to give voice to feminist spiritualities of struggle in this volume, keeping Divine Wisdom as the hermeneutical horizon and her power to bring justice about as the principle of cohesion. Seen from the plurality of contexts in which we live, the traditions of critical Wisdom seem to contain an appropriate and relevant language for expressing the motivations and intentions of our existence. Following the insights of Elisabeth Schüssler Fiorenza,[8] I find that this language enables us to: (1) prompt us to more critical analyses of our current historical situation, so as to see it honestly in its global systemic conformation and to face up to the multiple and varied domination of its kyriocentric systems; (2) fortify the several feminist spaces in which we not only seek to understand and explain this situation critically but also to change it radically, so as to achieve genuine justice and true well-being for women and for the human race as a whole; (3) contribute to the formation of a global Wisdom-community that will uphold our hopes, visions, and feminist struggles for a different civilization, one in which the relationships of human beings among themselves and with their environment may be constantly guided and sustained by the liberating Power of Divine Wisdom/Justice.

Finally, to close my reflection, I should like briefly to bring out some dimensions that illustrate our ideas and understandings of the feminist spiritualities of Wisdom. I have selected these dimensions on the basis of the various contributions to this volume, but I should like to stress that they are not the only ones, nor are they limited by closed definitions. I am speaking here of dimensions that express the living, dynamic, evolving, and committed character of these spiritualities.

I. Understandings

Feminist spiritualities of Wisdom are needed for the survival of our race and that of the world we live in. They provide us with a framework of reference that helps us to: understand and exercise the freedom Divine Wisdom infuses into us, with which we can choose liberating and humanizing relationships; discern and opt for a worthy, worth-giving, and just life; confront and change our situations in the direction of the aims of liberation; celebrate the hopes and motivations that accompany our struggles. In these spiritualities we find courage, inspiration, direction, and meaning to our lives. As opposed to kyriarchal spiritualities, which have brought the human race to certain death, feminist spiritualities bring us to life in accordance with the justice and mercy of Divine Wisdom.

II. Starting point

Feminist spiritualities of Wisdom accept that Divine Wisdom is present and at work, giving her understanding and inspiration to all.[9] Nevertheless, they deliberately construct their language on the basis of the experience of those who suffer under, stand up to, and struggle against the kyriarchal powers that operate in societies and religions. This leads them to see that the varied experiences of women, reflected on critically, come to be the central starting point in articulating our spiritualities.

III. Expressions

Feminist spiritualities of Wisdom have emerged, and are still doing so, in varied socio-cultural environments. These spiritualities use the resource of the symbolic, metaphorical, linguistic, and imaginative riches of various cultures, but they incorporate these riches in feminist terms. The varied expressions acquired by the spirituality of Wisdom have a constant element in a dynamic relationship with people's daily lives. These spiritualities arise from the circumstances of our daily lives and return to them in critical and creative tension. Starting from the daily occurrences of our existence, we seek to bring about and express transformation of ourselves and 'the system'. In this sense, feminist spiritualities of Wisdom have an inter-cultural vocation.

IV. Commitments

Feminist spiritualities of Wisdom declare their interests and their aims. They know that the power of spirituality is to set people free, not to keep them in resignation, paralysis, despair, or victimization. These spiritualities develop understandings, practices, and visions that have transforming effects in the direction of greater justice, well-being, equality, human dignity, and integrity for women, for the whole human race and the whole of creation. Therefore, these spiritualities understand and take on the ethical-political content of spirituality.

V. Celebrations

Feminist spiritualities of Wisdom engender an unceasing creativity in forms of celebrating all manifestations of life linked to our varied contexts of struggle. These manifestations include silences, tears, fears, breaks, and deep frustrations. We celebrate everything we do in our homes and in the streets to rebuild and give liberating power to what Mary Shawn Copeland calls 'our despised identities'.[10] We celebrate the memory of innumerable women who have bequeathed us visions of a new world, and we make spaces for festival here, where kyriarchal spiritualities bring only sadness.

VI. Towards the future in the Power of Wisdom

Feminist spiritualities of Wisdom are spiritualities seen as dangerous by the priests of the kyriarchal powers. These spiritualities are censured and persecuted owing to the simple fact that they seek justice and respect for people's human dignity. These spiritualities give us strength to go on imagining, resisting, and struggling. Because our commitment leads us to risk all that we are and have, we believe that feminist spiritualities can originate only in Divine Wisdom herself. We walk towards the future of a new world in the Power of Wisdom.

Translated by Paul Burns

Notes

1. The meaning of the term 'kyriarchy' can be found in several works by Elisabeth Schüssler Fiorenza. See especially *But She Said. Feminist Practices of Biblical Interpretation*, Boston: Beacon Press 1992, chs 1 and 4; *Jesus: Miriam's Child, Sophia's Prophet. Critical Issues in Feminist Christology*, New York: Continuum and London: SCM Press 1995, chs 1 and 3; 'Ties that Bind: Domestic Violence Against Women' in M. J. Mananzan et al. (eds), *Women Resisting Violence. Spirituality for Life*, Maryknoll: Orbis Books 1996, 39–55; *Rhetoric and Ethic. The Politics of Biblical Studies*, Minneapolis: Fortress Press 1999, Intro. and chs 3 and 4.
2. Schüssler Fiorenza, *But She Said*, 13, 156.
3. M. Fontenla and M. Bellotti, 'Feminismo y Neoliberalismo' in *la Correa Feminista*, <http://www.nodo50.org/mujeres/feminismo-neoliberalismo.html>.
4. See her *Jesus: Miriam's Child*.
5. F. J. Hinkelammert, 'Determinismo y autoconstitución del sujeto: Las leyes que se imponen a espaldas de los actores y el orden por el desorden' in *Pasos* 64 (Mar.-Apr. 1996), 18.
6. See the excellent A.-M. Portugal and C. Torres (eds), *El Siglo de las Mujeres*, Santiago de Chile 1999.
7. On the idea of 'daily life/daily affairs' see M. P. Aquino, 'Theological Method in US Latino/a Theology: Toward an Intercultural Theology for the Third Millennium' in O. O. Espín and M. H. Díaz (eds), *From the Heart of Our People:*

Latino/a Explorations in Catholic Systematic Theology, Maryknoll: Orbis Books
       1999, 38–39.

8. Although these dimensions are present in virtually all Schüssler Fiorenza's
   works, see especially *Bread Not Stone. The Challenge of Feminist Biblical
   Interpretation*, Boston: Beacon Press 1984, chs 1 and 6; *Discipleship of Equals. A
   Critical Feminist Ekklesia-logy of Liberation*, New York: Crossroad and London:
   SCM Press 1993; *Jesus: Miriam's Child*, chs 5 and 6. These dimensions run
   right through her inspiring *Rhetoric and Ethic*.

9. On this see *Rhetoric and Ethic*, 6, 53.

10. M. Shawn Copeland, 'Method in Emerging Black Catholic Theology' in D. L.
    Hayes and C. Davis (eds), *Taking Down Our Harps. Black Catholics in the United
    States*, Maryknoll: Orbis Books 1998, 121.

Contributors

ELISABETH SCHÜSSLER FIORENZA is Krister Stendahl Professor at Harvard Divinity School, Massachusetts. She is a past president of the Society of Biblical Literature and founding editor of the *Journal of Feminist Studies in Religion*; she is committed to Women-Church. Her most recent books are *In Memory of Her: A Feminist Reconstruction of Early Christian Origins*, *The Book of Revelation: Judgment and Justice*, *Bread not Stone: The Challenge of Feminist Biblical Interpretation* and *Jesus: Miriam's Child, Sophia's Prophet*.

Address: The Divinity School, Harvard University, 451 Francis Avenue, Cambridge, MA 02138, USA.

NAMI KIM was born and grew up in Seoul, South Korea, where she received her undergraduate degree from Ewha Women's University. She participated in the Study/Action program at the Women's Theological Center in Boston through 1992–93. After graduating from Candler School of Theology at Emory University in 1996, she has been working on her doctoral degree in Religion, Gender, and Culture at Harvard Divinity School.

Address: 40 Henry Street, #1, Medford, MA 02155, USA.

MARY E. HUNT is a feminist theologian from the Roman Catholic tradition active in the Women-Church movement. She is co-founder and co-director of the Women's Alliance for Theology, Ethics and Ritual (WATER), an educational organization in Silver Spring, Maryland, USA. She is an adjunct faculty member of the Women's Studies Program at Georgetown University. She is author of *Fierce Tenderness: A Feminist Theology of Friendship*.

Address: Women's Alliance for Theology, Ethics and Ritual (WATER), 8035 13th Street, Silver Spring, MD 10910, USA.
Email: mhunt@hers.com

IVONE GEBARA is a Brazilian feminist philosopher and theologian. She lives in the north east of Brazil and since 1990 has worked as an assessor for women's movements, particularly among the urban and rural poor. She is also visiting professor at several educational centres and universities in Latin America, North America and Europe. She is the author, with Maria-Clara Bingemer, of *Mary. Mother of God and Mother of the Poor* (ET 1993), and her latest book, *Le mal au féminin* (1999), has been translated into Portuguese and German.

Address: Rua Luiz Jorge dos Santos 278, Tabatinga, 54756–380 Camaragibe – PE, Brazil.

DIANN L. NEU has an STM and M.Div. from the Jesuit School of Theology at Berkeley, California, and an MSW from The Catholic University of America in Washington, DC. She is co-founder and co-director of WATER, the Women's Alliance for Theology, Ethics and Ritual, in Silver Spring, Maryland. Her publications include *Liturgia* (1997), *Women-Church Source-book* (1993, with Mary E. Hunt), *Women-Church Celebrations* (1989) and *Women of Fire* (1990, with Mary E. Hunt). She is a licensed psychotherapist, spiritual director and feminist liturgist who practises in the Washington, DC, area. She co-ordinates the Women-Church Convergence, lectures internationally, and is presently engaged in writing *WATER Spirit*, a three-volume series of feminist liturgies.

Address:WATER, 8035 13th Street, Silver Spring, MD 20910, USA.

MERCEDES NAVARRO PUERTO was born in Jerez in Spain in 1951 and is a Mercedarian Sister of Charity. She holds doctorates in psychology from Salamanca and in theology from the Gregorianum. She lectures in Old Testament and Psychology of Religion at the pontifical universities of Salamanca and Comillas and also practises as a psychotherapist. She has published books and articles on the Bible, psychology of religion, gender issues and Mariology. Her works include *Barro y aliento* (Earth and Breath, 1993); *Para comprender el cuerpo de la mujer* (Understanding Woman's Body, 1995); 'The Religious Experience of Women: Psychological Reflections in a Spanish Context' in A. Eser, A. Hunt Overzee and S. Roll (eds), *Revisioning Our Sources: Women's Spirituality in European Perspectives* (1997); and *Perspectiva psicológica de los fundamentalismos* (1999).

Address: Manipa 72, E-28027 Madrid, Spain.

SILVIA SCHROER was born in 1958. A Catholic theologian, she is Professor of Old Testament and the Biblical World in the Protestant Theological Faculty of the University of Berne. She has written numerous books and articles on the iconography of Palestine and Israel in the ancient Near Eastern world and on feminist exegesis.

Address: Evangelisch-Theologische Fakultät, Unitobler, Länggastrasse 51, CH 3000 Bern 9, Switzerland.

SUSAN STARR SERED is Associate Professor of Anthropology at Bar Ilan University, and currently serves as Acting Director of the Women's Studies in Religion Program at the Harvard Divinity School. Her research interests include fieldwork in Israel and in Okinawa (Japan). Her newest book is entitled *What Makes Women Sick?: Maternity, Modesty, and Militarism in Israeli Society*.

CAROL P. CHRIST is the author of *Rebirth of the Goddess* (Routledge 1998), the first feminist thealogy. She is Director of Ariadne Institute for the Study of Myth and Ritual, a non-profit organization that sponsors 'Goddess Pilgrimages to Crete' and 'Women's Quest in Lesvos'. She has been active in the feminist, peace, and environmental movements for over thirty years. She is working on a book of songs, prayers, and touchstones for the New Millennium, tentatively titled *Wisdom for Personal and Planetary Healing*.

Address: Molivos 81108, Lesbos, Greece.

MARY T. CONDREN was born in Hull and studied at the University of Hull, Boston College and Harvard University, where she graduated with a doctorate in Religion, Gender and Culture. She is the author of many articles on feminist theory, spiritual and liberation theology and written *The Serpent and the Goddess: Women, Religion and Power in Celtic Ireland*, London 1989. She is currently the Director of the Institute for Feminism and Religion in Ireland, the aim of which is 'to reclaim religion by engaging theoretically and experientially with the issues of feminist theology, ritual, spirituality and ethics'. She is a Research Associate in Women's Studies at Trinity College, Dublin.

Address: 3a Parkhlll Rise, Kilmanagh, Dublin 24, Ireland.

SILVIA REGINA DE LIMA SILVA lectures at the Biblical University of Latin America in Costa Rica. She is also a researcher for the DEI (Department of Ecumenical Research) there. She holds a doctorate in Biblical Sciences and specializes in theology and pastoral care for women. She has published articles on Black theology and feminist theology.

Address: Universidad Bíblica Latinoamericana, Apartado 901–1000, San José, Costa Rica.

MARÍA PILAR AQUINO is a Mexican-*Mestiza* Catholic theologian. She is Associate Professor of Theology and Religious Studies and Associate Director of the Center for the Study of Popular Catholicism at the University of San Diego. She earned her doctorate in theology at the Pontifical University of Salamanca, Spain (1991); the University of Helsinki, Finland, conferred on her the doctorate in theology *Honoris Causa* (2000). She is the author of *Our Cry for Life. Feminist Theology from Latin America* (1993); *La Teología, La Iglesia y La Mujer en América Latina* (1994); the editor of *Aportes para una Teología desde la Mujer* (1988), and co-editor of *Theology: Expanding the Borders*, with Roberto S. Goizueta (1998), and *Entre la Indignación y la Esperanza. Teología Feminista Latinoamericana*, with Ana María Tepedino (1998). She has published numerous articles on the feminist theological experience of the US Latina and Latin American communities.

Address: Department of Theology and Religious Studies, University of San Diego, 5008 Alcalá Park, San Diego, CA 02110.

CONCILIUM

Concilium Subscription Information

Issues published in 2001

February 2001/1: *God: Experience and Mystery*
edited by Werner Jeanrond and Christoph Theobald

April 2001/2: *The Return of the Just War*
edited by María Pilar Aquino Vargas and Dietmar Mieth

June 2001/3: *The Oecumenical Constitution of Churches*
edited by Oscar Beozzo and Giuseppe Ruggieri

October 2001/4: *Islamophobia*
edited by Elisabeth Shüssler Fiorenza and Karl-Josef Kuschel

December 2001/5: *Globalization and its Victims*
edited by Jon Sobrino and Felix Wilfred

New subscribers: to receive *Concilium 2001* (five issues) anywhere in the world, please copy this form, complete it in block capitals and send it with your payment to the address below.

Please enter my subscription for Concilium 2001

☐ Individual **£25.00/**US$50.00 ☐ Institutional **£35.00/**US$75.00

Issues are sent by air to the USA; please add £10/US$20 for airmail dispatch to all other countries (outside Europe).

☐ I enclose a cheque payable to SCM-Canterbury Press Ltd for £/$ ....

☐ Please charge my MasterCard/Visa   Expires ....

...................../............................/............................/............................

Signature ....

Name/Institution ....

Address ....

....

....

Telephone ....

Concilium SCM Press 9–17 St Albans Place London N1 0NX England
Telephone (44) 20 7359 8033 Fax (44) 20 7359 0049
E-mail: scmpress@btinternet.com

Printed in the USA
CPSIA information can be obtained
at www.ICGtesting.com
JSHW010916101223
53448JS00022B/229